CLINICAL PSYCHOLOGY REFLECTIONS VOLUME 5

CONNOR WHITELEY

No part of this book may be reproduced in any form or by any electronic or mechanical means. Including information storage, and retrieval systems, without written permission from the author except for the use of brief quotations in a book review.

This book is NOT legal, professional, medical, financial or any type of official advice.

Any questions about the book, rights licensing, or to contact the author, please email connorwhiteley@connorwhiteley.net

Copyright © 2024 CONNOR WHITELEY

All rights reserved.

DEDICATION

Thank you to all my readers without you I couldn't do what I love.

INTRODUCTION

Clinical psychology is an amazing area of psychology. It can improve lives, transform them and save people for the better, and it can decrease psychological distress too. That's why I love this great area of psychology.

However, the problem with how clinical psychology is taught in lecture theatres and formal education is that there are only so many topics you can teach, only so many debates you can talk about and there is only so much research in the world so you cannot have lively, heated debates at university.

I wanted somewhere to address this issue.

Therefore, I decided to write these clinical psychology reflection books where I can use evidence and research and my own fact-based opinions to explore some of the hottest debates in clinical psychology. As well as explore other topics from a clinical psychology perspective.

All these books are extremely fun to write and

are fascinating so I know you're going to enjoy them as well. Also, this has to be the best book in the series so far, because it explores topics in a lot more depth and we tackle some truly thought-provoking topics that impact the highest levels of clinical psychology practice and research.

If you're looking for an engaging, fascinating and easy-to-understand book exploring the edges of clinical psychology as well as other topics that you would never be taught at university, then this is the book for you.

You won't regret buying this book.

Who Am I?

Personally, I always love to know who the author is of the nonfiction I read so I know the information is coming from a good source. In case you're like me, I'm Connor Whiteley, the internationally bestselling author of over 40 psychology books.

In addition, I am the host of *The Psychology World Podcast,* a weekly show exploring a new psychology topic each week and delivering the latest psychology news. Available on all major podcast apps and YouTube.

Finally, I am a psychology graduate studying a Clinical Psychology Masters at the University of Kent, England.

So now we know more about each other, let's dive into some great clinical psychology reflections.

RETURNING TO CLINICAL PSYCHOLOGY AS A NEW PERSON

To kick off this 5th clinical psychology reflection book, I really want to explore a very personal topic in relation to clinical psychology. If you've read one of these books before or you're familiar with me, then you know I champion and encourage people with lived experiences of mental health conditions to go into clinical psychology. Due to we need people with lived experiences of therapy, mental health difficulties and more in the profession to help comfort and support our clients.

However, when I started my clinical psychology Masters with a lecture on the theory and introductory information to my Masters, I realised that I am coming back to clinical psychology as a completely different person to who I was during my undergraduate degree.

For context, I am now very much of the people with lived experiences and I always have been but I have been firmly denying my abuse and trauma up until the August of 2023.

What happened was that for about a decade I've been going through prolonged and intense emotional and verbal abuse in the form of homophobia from family and my general social environment. Then add in a number of traumatic events in-between that led to extremely bad mental health that I was never able to deal with, I really shouldn't have been surprised that I was going to have a mental health breakdown at some point.

That happened in August 2023 where I resumed a number of extremely negative coping mechanisms and I basically burnt my life to the ground because all my pain and suffering from a decade of abuse and trauma then exploded.

I simply couldn't continue living as I was so I changed my life forever, I went to therapy and I basically gave my family and friends an ultimatum in a fashion. Love me and support me or get out of my life.

Thankfully, they chose the love and support route which I am extremely grateful for because I do love them and I didn't want to lose them.

Anyway, I talk more about this in my memoir *Healing: A Gay Man's Journey to Happiness, Joy and Recovery From Abuse and Trauma*. In the book I go into the details of my struggles, what happened to me, my therapy sessions and how I recovered.

Therefore, I was sitting in my lectures

surrounded by 30 other Masters students and some of them were talking about their experiences of mental health difficulties. For instance, I know one person in the cohort has experience with domestic violence and another person has experience with extreme anxiety.

Then it just hit me that I was one of these students too now. I have lived experience of abuse, trauma and what it's like to go through therapy.

And I don't know but there was just something rather unsettling about that realisation. I think it comes from me having to admit that everything happened and me having to acknowledge all the pain, suffering and all the ways that my life is better after the summer.

However, as we went through the lecture, there was something about the language that other psychology students were using that started to annoy me a lot. Long time readers of the series know I always like talking about the importance of language within clinical psychology, but this was starting to annoy me.

I have never been a fan of the term mental health "problems" because that is very blaming. You are basically saying to a client that their depression, anxiety, suicidal ideation is their problem and they shouldn't burden anyone else with it.

That is what the term "problem" means because in life, if you have a problem then *you* need to fix it.

Instead myself and a lot of other clinical psychologists prefer the term "mental health difficulty" because it is a lot less blaming. We all have difficulties and we can all support each other with whatever we find difficult.

Anyway, we were talking in the lecture and the more the term "problem" was thrown about, the more annoyed I got. Since yes, I have been suicidal (and before you ask I would never ever ever do it), I have self-harmed and I have suffered extreme trauma at the hands of other people.

But does that make *me* a problem?

Of course not.

I am not a "problem" that needs to be solved and fixed and cured. Sure, you might argue that the ways that I dealt with my abuse and trauma was problematic and they could be considered "problems" in their own right. Yet even then if we say those coping mechanisms were problems then there is a very real risk a client would see themselves as a problem.

That isn't good in terms of psychotherapy.

As a result, I just hate the term "problem" because it isn't helpful, it makes a client feel bad about themselves and it doesn't help us, as current or future therapists, to create a space, welcoming space were clients can come and reveal their deepest, darkest secrets to us.

I am so grateful that my therapist didn't call my or my coping strategies a "problem" because I know I would have been more likely to shut down. Instead she was welcoming, friendly and she didn't judge me for one moment.

And as much as we bang on about being non-judgemental in clinical psychology, when we use words like "problems" and "disorder" that is exactly what we are doing. We are judging our clients, calling them problems and making them feel like crap when they have gathered up the courage to come and see us. Something that would have terrified them.

Overall, I am rather excited for the rest of the lectures, modules and discussions that will happen over the course of my Masters. Not only because I love clinical psychology and I am always excited to learn more, but because now I have lived experiences so I can understand and comment on different topics I learn about from both a psychology student's and a person with lived experience's perspective.

Something I fully believe will be invaluable and interesting and maybe even a little annoying in the future.

And even if you don't have lived experience of mental health difficulties, still love, learn and study clinical psychology because we still need amazing people like you. Just make sure that you listen to other people whenever they talk about lived experience because you never know how valuable that information will be in the future.

It's always better to know information and not need it than need information and not have it.

HELPING YOURSELF BY HELPING OTHERS

Every so often I like to write a reflection that isn't aimed at mental health or clinical psychology in particular, and this is one of those reflections because the "problem" with clinical psychology is that there is a good chance you will experience burnout at some point. Having to deal with tons of people with various mental health conditions, hearing the horrible and tragic things that happen to them and having to deal with the impossible working conditions all leads to a high chance of burnout at some point.

That's why it is even more important in clinical psychology that everyone looks after themselves and that is the angle that I'm working from in this reflection since volunteering can have a lot of great mental health benefits.

For example, research shows that volunteering decreases depression and increases self-esteem, happiness, life satisfaction and physical health (Thoits

& Hewitt, 2001). As well as a massive European study shows that volunteering can help people have the health benefits of a person five years younger than themselves (Detollenaere et al., 2017).

Also, research shows that people who volunteer have better mental and physical health, have more sense of purpose and increased general wellbeing (McDonald et al., 2013). As well as they have lower mortality risks, better cognitive health and better social and emotional functioning (Shmotkin et al., 2003).

Therefore, as you can see there are a lot of great reasons why we should all volunteer more.

In the rest of the chapter, I'm going to expand on this a little more, link it to clinical psychologists and comment on some of the challenges to volunteering because that is something important to acknowledge.

Personally, even though I haven't done any form of volunteering in about five, six years. I did enjoy it a lot. I was involved in Scouts for over a decade and I did a lot of volunteering through them and I did work with organisations like Youth United Foundation, went to King Charles's 70th Birthday Party (he was Prince back then) and I went to Malta with the Scouts too to work on an EU project.

Volunteering does present a lot of fun opportunities that I never would have gotten to do normally. As well as I know I only got these opportunities because of the amazing Scout leader who knew I was very capable and responsible. Hence there is a privilege element here which I will talk about later on.

Overall, the entire point is that volunteering is valuable, great and it honestly does make you feel like you are making a positive difference in the world.

Consequently, if we link this to clinical psychology then it is important that maybe those working in the profession do actually start volunteering more. They get involved in local projects, local groups and local campaigns to help them get these mental health benefits.

Then maybe this will start to decrease the high rate of burnout and psychological distress in the profession. Volunteering could help psychologists to relax after a hard day or week at the office and they might feel like they are more than their work, because of how overwhelming being a psychologist can be at times.

I know that working in clinical psychology settings can be exhausting, overwhelming and extremely tiring. Volunteering could help psychologists get back that positive attitude, feeling of control over their life and improved mental health that has probably been negatively impacted by their work in the past week.

Also, it is very much worth noting that being affected by what clients have to say is completely normal, it is to be expected and it really doesn't make a psychologist a bad one. It doesn't make them bad psychologist material, a weak person or any of that rubbish.

To have a reaction to the heart-breaking stories a psychologist has to hear at times is normal, and it makes them human.

Therefore, we do have to acknowledge that volunteering isn't perfect for everyone and there are systemic reasons for this, because people do need to be supported to volunteer. Especially in a high-demand, high-stress and full-time profession like clinical psychology.

Since most clinical psychologists I've spoken to work a full day, have a long or longish commute then they have to make dinner, do their housework, spend time with their kids if they have any and do X, Y and Z before bedtime.

Where's the time to volunteer during the week? There isn't any.

When it comes to the weekend, you probably want to relax, catch up with your family, your kids, spend time with your partner and just not do volunteering. I completely understand that and hell, I would be no different at all.

Even more important is that Poulin (2014) did some interesting research on how sometimes people volunteer to hide and manage the stressful life events that plague them in their personal life or work life. This very much sounds applicable to clinical psychology because of our high-stress and high-demand job.

This isn't a healthy way really to go about work-related stress. Instead we, as a group or profession, should be trying to help and manage work-related stress and decrease it so no one is experiencing a lot of stress at work, because that only makes burnout more likely.

Therefore, we have to be wary of that and we need to acknowledge that as a profession, we have a good way to go in helping to make the clinical psychology workplace less stressful for workers.

Although, I have to admit I sort of think this is outside of our control. Since until governments, NHS bosses and more make a concrete effort to decrease workload and improve working conditions, we are very stuck in our workplace at the moment.

I could be wrong, but I doubt it.

A final point to note is privilege because not everyone has the same opportunities to volunteer as everyone else. Two simple reasons are that a single mother couldn't volunteer like a rich, wealthy couple raising kids. Equally, people from lower socioeconomic backgrounds are less likely to have the resources to volunteer their time for free.

For example, middle class people compared to lower class people have more time and resources to dedicate to volunteering (Sundeen et al., 2007). As well as there could be a perception amongst richer people that they need to help the lower, poorer people as a way of a "needy others" handout. This reinforces power inequalities and perceptions about lower-class people, and it could make lower-class people resent the volunteers (Ganesh & McAllum, 2009).

Overall, there are a lot of great and powerful benefits for people who volunteer and I do think that clinical psychologists, if they can, should take up volunteering because it could really help them maintain their mental health and decrease burnout. Yet volunteering isn't as easy as you think and there are barriers to volunteering that we have to overcome.

In time I really hope we will work out a way to overcome these barriers, but until then we need to be aware of them and try to think of ways to combat them, so everyone can enjoy the great benefits that volunteering brings to our lives, our communities and most importantly, our mental health.

References

Sundeen, R. A., Raskoff, S. A., & Garcia, M. C. (2007). Differences in perceived barriers to volunteering to formal organizations: Lack of time versus lack of interest. *Nonprofit Management and Leadership*, *17*(3), 279-300.

Ganesh, S., & McAllum, K. (2009). Discourses of volunteerism. *Annals of the International Communication Association*, *33*(1), 343-383.

Poulin, M. J. (2014). Volunteering predicts health among those who value others: Two national studies. *Health Psychology*, *33*(2), 120.

Thoits, P. A., & Hewitt, L. N. (2001). Volunteer work and well-being. *Journal of health and social behavior*,

115-131.

Detollenaere, J., Willems, S., & Baert, S. (2017). Volunteering, income and health. *PloS one*, *12*(3), e0173139.

McDonald, T. W., Chown, E. L., Tabb, J. E., Schaeffer, A. K., & Howard, E. K. (2013). The impact of volunteering on seniors' health and quality of life: An assessment of the retired and senior volunteer program. *Psychology*.

Shmotkin, D., Blumstein, T., & Modan, B. (2003). Beyond keeping active: Concomitants of being a volunteer in old-old age. *Psychology and aging*, *18*(3), 602.

AN UPDATE ON HOW ANGER DRIVES ACTION

I have to admit that this is a very interesting reflection for a few reasons even before we start talking about the topic itself. Since out of the five reflection books so far, I have never ever really "revisited" a reflection before, but this is a critical topic that I want to reflect on again. It is very important for reasons I will talk about in a moment.

Another reason why this is an interesting reflection is twofold. Firstly, this is one of the reflections that I wrote long before I wrote the rest of this book, which is weird in itself. Secondly, I had massive procrastination problems with this reflection as it is so personal and important to me that I really didn't want to write it for the longest of time.

Now let's talk about what this reflection actually means.

What Is How Anger Drives Action?

Back in Volume 4 of the series, I wrote about how anger drives us, as humans, towards doing some kind of action. And how anger isn't actually a bad thing if we use it in a positive way since anger can be a very, very powerful force for good.

Below is a 463-word extract from the longer reflection in the last volume, and I've included it because it gives a real flavour for why anger is a force for good. In the reflection itself, I did include a clinical psychology focus, but I will explore that angle anew in this reflection.

Enjoy.

"For example, if we start off generally before narrowing in on clinical psychology, the world is filled with anger and injustice at times, and at least that is what the news definitely makes us feel at times. And whilst the news is designed to get a rise out of us and make us angry, it isn't always a bad thing that anger turns into action.

It is bad if we watch something on the news for example and that drives us to violently protest, smash up shops and burn down buildings. That is wrong, but equally I do understand that certain things do provoke enough strong emotion to drive people to do that sort of thing. As well as like always the debate about right and wrong is subjective and very much beyond the scope of this book.

Yet if we look towards anger bringing about positive change and action then this has always been the case throughout history, or at least modern history. For instance, if black people and LGBT+ people didn't get annoyed, feed-up and outraged by their constant mistreatment, murder and being treated differently from other law-abiding citizens. Then this never would have led to the stonewall riots, what Rosa Parks did and the events that followed and everything that allows civil rights and equality to function today. That was in the 60s and onwards.

Then if we go back even further towards the start of the 20th century with the suffragettes and the suffragists (the difference is very interesting so I do recommend researching it for yourself), then if women didn't get angry about their mistreatment and how they were barred from doing almost everything in society. Then women would never be allowed to vote, be more than mothers and be more than a mere sex object for men.

Of course I am flat out not saying that modern society is perfect because it's seriously not, but these are just some historical examples about how anger leads to positive action and change. Granted some of the suffragettes did have questionable methods at times.

Then this is still something we can see in society today from the peaceful climate change protests, to the protests surrounding Scottish Independence and the protests surrounding Black Lives Matter and more. All of these are peaceful for the vast, vast majority of the time and this all came from anger about a situation and people wanting to change it to improve their lives.

Overall, anger is a powerful force for good if used correctly and anger can definitely bring around a lot of good action that improves society. Of course at the time, these protests and these people are seen as crazy, weird and far-left nutters, but history thankfully remembers the suffragettes and others as heroes."

<u>Why Did I Want To Revisit This Topic?</u>

I've decided to revisit this reflection because of a lot of things that have been happening in my personal life lately, and I think there are a lot of lessons that I can apply to clinical psychology here. Even more so because a lot of the lessons themselves are based in clinical psychology.

Therefore, to start at the beginning, a few weeks ago as I write this, I went out with a friend of mine. He's a trans man and he's great. Really good friend, really nice guy and it is impossible not to like him.

Me and my friend had been talking for a while over Instagram ever since we met at a university Outreach event, and he wanted to have an in-person catch-up. So that happened, I had a great time and it was so nice to be another friend that I could just talk about things with that I simply couldn't talk about with my own family or other straight friends.

Later on, what happened was we continued to talk throughout the week afterwards, and I realised that because I have been looking at getting some work experience anyway. I already have my learning disability work experience in September 2023 but I wanted some more.

So I was thinking about working with trans people, because since meeting him I sort of fell down the rabbit hole of learning about it. Since honestly, it is really interesting to learn about and you quickly realise how all the anti-trans myths are complete and utter lies.

Anyway, I made myself leave the work experience alone in case I was just wanting to do it because I had had a nice time with my friend. I normally have a four-day rule, meaning if I'm still excited after four days I give myself permission to actually do it.

Now that weekend there was a lot of homophobia and transphobia at home and in my family more generally. As well as it was the same weekend that my friend, who was Latvian, was upset because Russia signed their stupid law banning legal and medical changes for transgender people. Meaning it negatively impacted how his extended family saw him.

And I am no stranger to homophobia, hate and bad mental health because of it. I seriously am not a stranger to it all.

However, this weekend caused me to be extremely, extremely angry, almost rageful I would say on the Monday and Tuesday. Now the nice thing about me being angry is I am passive aggressive to the extreme. It is honestly impossible for you to tell that I am angry because I do hide it.

It's a survival strategy that I learnt years ago.

Yet I was so angry and rageful, and it actually took me ages to realise why that was. Since as I mentioned earlier, intense hatred towards me isn't new at all, and I do realise that social psychology teaches us that our own self-knowledge is very, very poor. Still, go with me here because there is a clinical psychology point shortly.

On the whole, I think I was so angry because I had just had a great week of going out with my friend, talking to him through the week and just enjoying having an accepting friend that didn't judge me, hate me and most importantly, he understood me.

So when at the weekend I had to put up with even more homophobia than usual and I had a good friend that was upset too. I was just so angry that my family couldn't be supportive, happy and accepting towards me like my friend had (and to be honest everyone else at university).

Also, I think I was so angry because, whilst I am used to homophobia myself. I've come to realise in recent weeks that my life is all about helping people. Whether it is through providing knowledge and entertainment through my books and podcast, to me giving blood and being an organ donor to save lives. As well as me wanting to be a clinical psychologist in the future, I am happy to say that my life is all about helping people.

Meaning I don't like seeing or hearing other

people suffer.

Now I do realise that this makes me sound like a very emotional person, but I am seriously not. It is definitely one of the more interesting parts of being autistic, it doesn't exactly make you the most expressive of people. Except when I'm writing, like I would never say even a tenth of this reflection in public.

So I suppose that's a clinical psychology point straight away. This reflection helps you to understand the struggles and life of an autistic person.

In addition, another part of my autism is that I don't "care" about a lot of people. I like tons of people and I love my readers truly, but it is hard to explain. But there aren't a lot of people I would bend over backwards for or destroy my routine for.

That's a better way to explain it as routines are the lifeblood of autistic people.

Therefore, when I heard that my friend, which I do care about, was upset and everything else was going on was happening at the same time. This made me furious with my world, myself and my friend's parents as well as a ton of other people.

I was furious.

How I Used Anger To Drive Action?

Now, of course like any normal person, I could have simply allowed my anger that surprisingly enough lasted for two whole days to simply go away. And I did do that for the most part but I allowed my anger to cement my positions too on certain topics.

It made me believe even more how much I respect and are not bothered by trans people, because I can promise regardless of whatever the myths say. Trans people aren't nutters, they seriously are not doing this for attention and the trans community is a tiny, tiny portion of the population.

However, it also made me a lot more determined to do work experience and work with trans people, and I developed a real, real passion for this clinical population.

So much so that I actually surprised myself.

Since if you've been a long time reader of mine or a listener of The Psychology World Podcast then you know I flat out love clinical psychology and everything within the discipline. I do want to do clinical psychology, I want to help people and improve lives. Yet I have never ever felt as passionate and fired up about wanting to work with any clinical population than I did about trans people.

Meaning I set out to apply to a lot of public and private sector services that worked with clients with gender dysphoria. By the time, this reflection book comes out in 2025 I definitely should have done a lot of stuff on work experience and whatnot on The Psychology World Podcast. So if you're interested in work experience definitely check out the backlist of the podcast.

In total, I used a letter template that I adapted for each of the 13 places that I applied for, and I will admit I learnt a hell of a lot about trans people during my research for this work experience.

Nonetheless, my point about this section is that my anger drove me to spend a good few hours of the week of my anger to researching, writing out letters and submitting them to different organisations. Therefore, not only could I work with a clinical population I am extremely passionate about, but so I could continue to develop clinical skills (ideally in an NHS setting) that will benefit me in my future clinical psychology career.

<u>Over To You</u>

Overall, the entire point of this updated reflection was to show you a practical example of how being angry isn't a bad thing at all, if you use it in a positive manner. Therefore, if there is something that angers you about a clinical population, if there is an injustice in clinical psychology you want to sort out, or something else entirely. Then do something positive to help that clinical population.

Of course, you could argue that work experience with a clinical population doesn't help them. Maybe you're right, but it will still help you gain clinical experience, an understanding of how to work in clinical psychology and you never know the impact you will have on a client.

I always come to the realisation that therapy, a psychological assessment and formulations are always a scary, scary time for our clients. We are asking them to open up to us, complete strangers, and reveal things that society has told them are wrong, messed up and flat out weird.

You never know, your friendly face, your positive actions and your younger presence in the therapy room might be exactly what the client needs to feel more relaxed.

I don't know, but my point is never underestimate the positive contributions you can make to a clinical population if you want to.

I know not a lot of people will want to help trans people due to the awful social and political climate we find ourselves in, but even if I get a single week of work experience and I can make a positive impact on a single person's life. Then those hours of researching, writing up letters and submitting them will be more than worth it.

People in clinical psychology help people, improve lives and give people a future. And if you do it right, anger can certainly help with that ambition in very surprising and wonderful ways.

MENTAL HEALTH CONDITIONS AS REACTIONS

Whilst in the next chapter we're going to be focusing on this idea using trauma, I wanted to explore this fun idea I first heard in one of my undergraduate clinical psychology lectures. The idea comes from the psychological and socioconstructivist viewpoint that mental health conditions aren't strange, abnormal signs of madness like the biomedical model proposes but instead they are reasonable if not maladaptive reactions to different situations.

Now I will admit I love this idea because I think there is a large amount of truth to this idea. As well as this is why I like these reflective books because they allow me to reflect and use fact-based opinions to talk about some of these things.

Social Anxiety

Therefore, let's take anxiety as a first example and a young kid has a terribly embarrassing experience at a party that led to a lot of humiliation. This would cause any young person a lot of psychological distress and I wouldn't be surprised if this was a major cause if they went on to develop social anxiety disorder.

Okay, then we would have to ask ourselves if social anxiety could be a reaction to this feeling of psychological distress and the associated experience.

I think there is an argument to be made for it. I don't think anyone would like to be humiliated yet again in another social situation and experience high levels of psychological distress. Then if this person had other risk factors for social anxiety then I don't think it is a silly idea to propose that being socially anxious, rapid heartbreak, intense nervousness and panic attacks when going into a social situation, could be a reaction to this unpleasant event.

In addition, social anxiety could be a reaction even more if the negative experiences in social groups were repeated with different people and across time. Then if a person keeps having bad experiences (according to their perception of the event if we tap into the cognitive approach here) then I think being socially anxious and avoiding social groups is a reasonable reaction.

There isn't a particular point I'm trying to make here except that maybe mental health conditions aren't signs of madness, craziness and inadequate social functioning after all. Maybe they're just maladaptive reactions to bad situations.

Depression

For our second example, let's look at depression that is traditionally characterised as low mood, low energy and not getting as much pleasure from activities as you used to. Yes, I appreciate there are other symptoms of depression but still, this is an exploratory reflection to be honest so let's keep things relatively simple here.

A depressed person has negative automatic thoughts about themselves, others and the world after a particular event triggers their vulnerabilities, at least according to the Diathesis Stress model.

Therefore, for the sake of this reactions argument, the depression that is caused by the triggering event could be a maladaptive reaction to whatever happened. For example, I know one the major changes between the DSM-4 and 5 was now you can be diagnosed with depression if a loved one has died recently.

If the death of a loved one caused the person's depression vulnerabilities to express themselves. Then the low mood, low energy and loss of enjoyment could be a normal reaction to the loss of a loved one. I don't think any of us feel that great after a loved one dies, I know I don't.

Another factor to consider is one of the cognitive biases that reveal themselves in depressed people. For instance, depressed people generalise their failures so they might fail one subject at school and the depression makes them believe they'll fail everything at school. In terms of thinking about this as a reaction, I don't think it's futile to argue that if a depressed person fails at something and they already feel bad about themselves, isn't generalising a normal reaction to failing?

Is it actually any different to non-depressed people lecturing others about how they'll never find love after they experience a breakup?

Not really.

On the whole, of course this reaction argument isn't foolproof but I think it is a useful tool in helping us to realise that the maladaptive coping mechanisms and consequences of mental health difficulties are actually logical reactions to have in bad situations.

Mental health difficulties don't make a person bad, messed up or needing to be "cured". They are just trying to function in response to a bad situation and our clients need more adaptive and helpful ways to react in different situations.

This is another analogy we can use to explain this idea.

Post-Traumatic Stress Disorder

The final example I want to look at is PTSD because I think this is the clearest example of mental health conditions as a response to bad situations. Since PTSD develops when a person has been through trauma and they experience intense psychological distress, intrusive flashbacks and memories and they experience impaired functioning in different areas of their life.

Let's say a soldier went overseas and saw their friends ripped to shreds by a bomb and then they had to fight for survival, pinned down by the enemy for an hour until help arrived.

If seeing your friends ripped to shreds isn't trauma then I really don't want to know what is.

Leading to the soldier later developing PTSD with the symptoms I mentioned earlier. I forget the theory off the top of my head but I know there is literature on it, yet there is an argument that the intrusive memories and flashbacks are the mind trying to get the soldier to confront their past and deal with the trauma.

Therefore, in that sense the intrusive memories are a reaction to the trauma by the body because the mind wants to help the person deal with the past so they can move on with their life.

The psychological distress would be a reaction to the horror of the war, seeing their friends die in front of them and the stress of staying alive whilst waiting for help to arrive. The soldier would have spent that hour thinking that they were going to die, just imagine the horror and sheer stress that would have caused.

Finally, the impaired social functioning would be a consequence of the intrusive thoughts and memories and the distress caused by the trauma. Yet I still think (and know because of my own trauma experiences) that we all have to deal with trauma in our own ways and if we come across as socially awkward, rude or distant. Then they might be a reaction the soldier has to not wanting to get close to anyone again in case they get ripped to shreds like their last friends did.

In conclusion, I appreciate a lot of this chapter has been hypothetical discussions and theorising about different mental health conditions. There is no literature on this argument to the best of my knowledge, except the PTSD stuff, and I don't care enough to have a look.

However, my point is that in case you are of the persuasion and therapeutic orientation that believes people with mental health conditions are strange, abnormal and a little messed up. Then just start questioning this damaging and harmful belief because as someone with lived experience, I can promise you, we are just trying to survive in the world after experiencing bad stuff.

Sure the things people do with mental health conditions might be strange and confusing to other people but to a large extent, all the symptoms and consequences that we see in people with mental health conditions are just reactions and maladaptive coping mechanisms they use to get through the day and live.

One day at a time.

TRAUMA AS NORMAL REACTIONS TO ABNORMAL SITUATIONS

As we continue our look at a new way to look at maladaptive coping mechanisms and the different ways that our clients might show behaviours that are harmful to themselves and others, I want to use this reflection to focus in on trauma a little more using a more general approach to clinical psychology and then drawing on my own experience in the second half.

Therefore, there is a wide range of trauma and behaviours that a client can show. Some trauma might be caused from child abuse, violence, a car crash, being a soldier in a war zone, being victimised in a crime or going through secondary victimisation and so on.

There is a wide range of what can traumatise someone.

In addition, I think whilst there are a lot of similarities between trauma victims and survivors, there is room for variation too about their behaviour and the different ways that they cope. A lot of trauma survivors do have intrusive memories and thoughts, they have increased levels of anxiety and panic attacks when they encounter a situation similar to the traumatising one. As well as they show avoidance behaviours towards something that might remind that of their trauma.

However, there are differences in how they cope with the trauma. Some people might disassociate from the trauma completely, others might block out the memory, others might choose to partake in substance abuse, alcoholism and self-harm or suicidal ideation.

Furthermore, others might withdraw from the world as well.

All of these different maladaptive coping mechanisms are harmful, damaging and should be addressed in therapy whenever the client admits they need to change, and they have the capacity to change. Since we cannot help someone that doesn't want to change their ways.

Nonetheless, if we really think about it, none of these maladaptive coping mechanisms make a person crazy, insane or whacky. They are all reasonable reactions to abnormal situations.

I've already used the soldier example so let's use the example of a rape victim. Something that is extremely distressing, flat out outrageous and beyond disgusting. I have never really looked into rape trauma in any great depth so I might get small details wrong and I apologise for that, my expertise and experience lay with child abuse and trauma more, but my point will still be clear.

Therefore, if a person was raped at a university party by three men and the person was about to leave when it happened and they were raped in a dark alley. This might lead to the person becoming depressed, having social anxiety about parties and a fear of going out after dark, even more so if they live on the university campus. As well as to cope with the feelings of shame, guilt and helplessness that rape makes a person feel, they might start drinking excessively to black out the memories of the rape. As well as they might experience emotional numbness that makes them want to self-harm so they can feel something and punish themselves for the rape.

I know I've drawn on a lot of different concepts that I'm familiar with but I want to make a point now.

Normally we would see these behaviours as messed up, unhelpful and the drinking would bring a lot of stigma to the victim that a lot of people wouldn't be interested in helping them. Due to the strong stigma that alcoholism is associated with.

However, when we consider these behaviours through the lens of the person being a victim and the person going through the trauma of being raped. Then things start to make a lot more sense because if a person has gotten through something extremely traumatic causing them to have intrusive memories and they are constantly forced to think about the rape. Of course they are going to want to forget about it and block it out of their mind.

Hence, the alcoholism and it makes sense because alcohol can be used to help someone blackout and forget. It isn't healthy but still.

Furthermore, after going through the traumatic experience of rape attack at a party in the dark on a university campus (something for the sake of honesty is very uncommon) then it is reasonable to be socially anxious about parties, going out after dark and being on a university campus. You would want to engage in avoidance behaviours so the traumatic experience doesn't happen again and you don't have to go through it again.

In addition, if we think about trauma I know from experience that it is emotionally exhausting and I imagine (because mine was prolonged) that a single "short", sharp traumatic experience would be emotionally crippling and because the emotions would be too intense, too negative and too awful that a person would be emotionally numb after the experience.

And people want to feel good, they want to feel alive and they just want to feel something, anything. I know I felt like that after a month of my negative mental health.

Therefore, it is possible that self-harm might be an "attractive" option for the person so they can feel something. It would be painful and extremely unhealthy but it would allow them to feel a reaction and an emotion.

<u>Drawing On My Experience</u>

Before I conclude the reflection and explain why this is a powerful exercise to think about, I want to "briefly" draw on my own trauma experiences and why what I did were reasonable reactions to my situation.

I've mentioned before that my trauma experiences led me to self-harm, become emotionally closed off and experience suicidal ideation at times. As well as I've explained the context before so I'm not going to do that again.

Therefore, I used to self-harm because I could never get angry, shout and scream at my home environment whenever they would say "you need to beat the gay out of them", gay people should die and that all gay people are rapists and paedophiles. I couldn't fight them with words on these disgusting beliefs because I needed them more than they needed me, I needed their support for other aspects of my life, I needed shelter and food.

I was angry that my home environment (who didn't know I was gay) considered me a rapist and that I needed to die. I would be rageful at times, but I would internalise my rage because I couldn't disrupt the boat because I needed them.

So I would scratch myself until I bleed to get the anger out of me. I served its purpose, I felt like I was doing something useful with the anger and it made me feel okay.

The abnormal situation in this case was being told repeatedly, almost weekly for a decade that I needed to get beaten so my reaction was self-harm. And I have no doubt there was a punishment aspect to this self-harm too. Yet it was reasonable in my eyes to self-harm given the hate, shame and guilt that was constantly being thrown my way.

This connects to the suicide aspect too as a reaction, because my family and wider social network never would have supported me being gay and being me. They all believed that gay people were abominations, they were against God and they should have been beaten.

Just imagine hearing this about you time and time again, week after week for a decade.

Then throw in some other trauma from friendships and family problems as well as complications caused by undiagnosed autism then things get tense real quick. And I was completely alone to deal with all of it so I just wanted things to end so I could get a long moment of peace and quiet.

Therefore, the abnormal situation was the intense stress, fear and shame caused by the beliefs of my wider social network and family. So it would be reasonable to want to escape it all and want to die so I didn't have to deal with all this anymore.

I would never ever kill myself, but I used to want to.

Then the emotionally closed part was just a way

to cope with other violate and unstable friendships and close-to-legal things that happened during my life based on the lies and misunderstandings of others. Therefore, it is simpler not to be close to people so they couldn't hurt me anymore.

On the whole, I won't lie and say that self-harm and suicide aren't some of the most serious coping mechanisms you will see, but there are always reasons for them. No one wants to die but sometimes people feel like it is the only way out.

Thankfully, in reality, it never is.

The Entire Point Of This Reflection

Overall, the entire point of this exercise is to get us to realise that maladaptive coping mechanisms don't make our clients whackos, messed up or deranged. It is them trying to function after a traumatic experience that they don't know how to cope with.

Humans are designed to cope and survive and thrive no matter what. Sometimes we have to turn to "darker" means to do just that but everyone wants to survive and just live one day at a time. And if alcohol, self-harm and other extreme traumatic responses help them to do that then it is reasonable but something that has to be addressed in therapy at some point when the person realises they don't want to continue like this.

It's an empowering realisation for sure, I know that, but it takes a lot longer than it should but that's a reflection for another day perhaps.

A STATISTICS AND ARTIFICIAL INTELLIGENCE RANT AND HOW IT RELATES TO CLINICAL PSYCHOLOGY?

Considering by the end of this book, I would have done exactly 100 of these clinical psychology reflections, I am very impressed with myself that this is the only one that will ever be a rant. I know some of the other reflections might have seemed like I was having a go at something in the world or clinical psychology or something else related to mental health, but they weren't rants.

They were honestly me being passionate about something wrong with the world and how we needed to fix it to improve mental health.

Anyway, this is a full-on rant but it is very relevant and very important to the future of psychology education and clinical psychology in turn.

For the purposes of this chapter, I'll explain what happened and why this is important to talk about and then I want to dissect some of the examples my lecturer gave because they really annoyed me and I might even argue they are dangerous with possibly deadly consequences.

Let me explain.

So I had my first statistics lecture this week because I've started my clinical psychology Masters, and like always, the lecturer in the first week goes through all the introductory stuff. Yet this lecturer might have had a background in clinical psychology, but his "real" main background was in artificial intelligence.

Therefore, within the first hour of the lecture, he basically turned round and said to us something along the lines of "in a few years all this statistics stuff won't be needed because AI will do it and more,"

Okay then, I was not impressed as soon as he said that but let me explain what else he said so you can understand my frustration even more.

I am paraphrasing in this entire chapter but the point is scarily clear.

"AI will allow us to do more with data analysis and it will allow us to explore data in more depth than statistics allows us to,"

Why do I need to learn statistics then and why am I "paying" (with taxpayer money) to listen to you talk for four hours a week if I don't need this stuff?

Also and this is what really annoyed me and this is why even after two days I am writing this with a bit of anger.

"universities and employers want people who can code and can work with AI on their CVs. The university said to me, I got this lecturer job because I have experience with AI,"

What the fuck!

So the university in its infinite wisdom is not only making me and my cohort learn statistical knowledge that will be useless in a few years because AI will be so good (it is actually good enough now to be fair) and it will be so mainstream that AI will do the data analysis for me.

Also, the university isn't going to teach me about AI, it will not teach me coding and it will not teach me a whole host of other computing skills that the university itself has said employers want.

What is the fucking point of my statistics lectures?

Personally, I just do not believe there is a point even more so because I have no intention of working in the poorly paid, high stressed and abusive working environment of academia. I have no interest in working in computing or data science. I have no interest in any of that.

And yes, I know full well clinical psychologists need to know about statistics and research methods. Research is the lifeblood of clinical psychology after all.

But when a former clinical psychology turned academic preaches to an entire cohort saying that statistics won't be needed because of AI in the future,

I just don't know. I don't see the point in learning any of this except it allows me to pass my Masters.

That is it.

Nonetheless, in all fairness, the lecturer did mention that he asked the university about officially teaching psychology students about AI. The university said no for this year but they might next year onwards.

Again, not exactly useful considering I will not be at the university next year and I hope to be out in the psychology job market, but with several computer skills less than other graduates it seems.

And before anyone asks, I am too annoyed because of what I'll mention below to self-teach. As well as I am a psychology person, if I wanted to do computer programming I would have done a computer science degree, also I have trouble learning advance computer topics without someone teaching it to me. That's why I like having lectures about R because I tried self-teaching (granted I was having a mental breakdown at the time but still) and that just failed miserably.

However, my real problem with the AI revelations was the fact that his clinical psychology examples fucked me off.

The Problems With AI In Clinical Psychology

For the sake of ease and to give you a layman's explanation of how Artificial Intelligence works and how Machine Learning works, it takes millions of datapoints, creates a model to predict behaviour and then it gives you an outcome.

Firstly, there is one problem I have straight away. Behaviour is not something you can simply predict with 100% certainty. If that was the case then everyone that had ever been abused as a child should go into therapy because we know abused children are at an increased risk of developing mental health difficulties.

That is an increased risk, not an absolute.

We also know that when people are depressed, there is an increased risk of suicide. Again that is not an absolute.

Equally, I know from personal experience that someone who looks to have the perfect life, perfectly happy and has high school grades should seem like a clinically normal person. But fuck is that not the case at times.

Therefore, the very assumption that you can create an AI model that is more accurate than the current research and that model can predict behaviour more than a clinical psychologist, I just have trouble believing.

Especially because there is no causal research in mental health to be honest. We can say abuse may lead to an increase risk of self-harm and suicide but it cannot say with empirical certainty sexual abuse causes self-harm. Since it doesn't, people self-harm for tons of different reasons.

However, the main example my lecturer used and this is the only one that stuck in my mind because I was so annoyed by it, was he said that Machine Learning will allow us to predict exactly when clients are likely to commit suicide.

Again, there is that magic word "exactly" but I have already spoken about that.

I have no doubt that Artificial Intelligence based on the current research could create a model that is just as good as a clinical psychologist or maybe, maybe slightly better at predicting suicide risk with a client.

However, when it comes to a client and being assessed with suicide risk, the data put into the machine and into the model is not subjective. A client cannot know with 100% if they will commit suicide at a given time in a given week in a given situation. They might have intense feelings of suicidal ideation but they might not go through with it.

Also, the client is most certainly (notice I didn't use a more definitive statement) depressed so they have cognitive biases impacting their self-perception, knowledge and this is going to have an impact on the model. As well as this model will likely miss the human factor, the body language, the tone of voice and all those other small indicators that help form a part of the risk assessment that a human psychologist would do.

I know AI isn't about replacing human therapists, but still.

In addition, what about the clients like me when I had my mental health breakdown back in August

2023. I knew for a fact even when I was at my worse and I truly wanted to die, I knew I would never do it. I still know I wouldn't do it in the future and that's before I remember how great my life is now.

However, I can promise you according to all the research I've read over the years on suicide, I would be shocked if an AI model said I wasn't a suicide risk. Yet what would have happened if an AI model did say I was a suicide risk, would I be ripped away from my family? Would I be institutionalised? And if we're going to be extreme here, would I be drugged up so I was too docile to do anything?

Of course, I will admit I am taking the mick here, but these are all good questions. If an AI model believes someone is a suicide risk based on research and it lacks the human connection and human factor that a conversation with a therapist can bring. Then what will the consequence be?

I can promise all of you that if I was ripped away from my family, my life, my routines and I was placed in some strange environment that I didn't want to be in. That would only decrease my mental health even further and who knows, maybe I would have actually considered doing it for real.

There are consequences for giving people labels based on cold, hard science.

My last comment or example is about the sheer imperfection of the data we give mental health professionals. Since I went for a counselling assessment last week and I didn't like the woman doing it, she was too smiley and giggly and interrupting me. She asked if I had ever actually attempted suicide, and if I had liked her, I would have told her the truth saying "No but there have been three times in my life when I have actively wanted to and come very close to actually making an attempt". Yet I didn't like her and I didn't trust her so I simply said no.

If that simple "No" had been plugged into an AI model then its risk assessment of me would be completely different.

When it comes to gathering data and information in clinical psychology so much of it depends on the client, the therapist and their therapeutic interaction. And clients might feel uncomfortable talking about certain things for a while so they might bend the truth, the therapist might realise this, but would an AI model?

I simply have no idea because the university refuses to teach us about AI at this moment in time.

And I certainly think that this is when clinical psychology becomes as much an artform than a science. We absolutely have to listen to the science about how to improve mental health and create an intervention that will almost certainly work. Yet our clients are individuals, random variables of data and they are amazing in their own right.

I think if we boil them down to pieces of data to feed into a model then we are betraying everything clinical psychology has been trying to build since its creation. We are moving towards a place in our profession that focuses on individualised formulation that puts the client as an individual at the heart of everything we do.

And if we see them as data then, as someone who has been through hell and back, then that is a fucking disgrace and that is unforgivable in my opinion.

TRANSFORMATION THROUGH TRAUMA

In the April 2023 issue of The Psychologist magazine, there was a brilliant article or book recommendation or something that spoke about how trauma can be a positive transformation experience after recovery, and I love the framing of this recovery.

Since as long-term readers and listeners of my books and podcast probably know by now, I am a positive person that focuses on helping people, I like modern thinking and I like being positive about mental health conditions and extremely negative experiences, including trauma because of my own experiences.

Therefore, I do want to take the time here to help show you that trauma might be extremely negative and it can result in a ton of negative mental health outcomes for an individual. Yet there is a great sense of hope and exploration and transformation that comes from trauma too.

Of course, the ideal situation is for a person never ever to go through any trauma in the first place, but sadly that just isn't possible. Especially, for certain sexual, racial and gender minorities as well as certain jobs like being a soldier.

I strongly believe this is an important reflection for us, as future or current clinical psychologists, because we understand the importance of trauma-informed practice and we are starting to understand that through formulation and the biopsychosocial model as well as the cognitive approach to mental health, that it is our perceptions and societal beliefs that impact our mental health too.

This is certainly true when it comes to trauma, because if society somewhat rightly tells someone trauma is *only* negative and there is no hope for them then the client will believe it. And even if they do thankfully seek professional help and the therapy works, they might miss the transformational aspects of trauma.

Furthermore, I tend to find there are two board types of trauma recovery and regaining a sense of identity after trauma recovery. There is returning to the identity you had before the traumatic event if you had a stable identity beforehand.

Or if you had childhood trauma and abuse like me then the question of identity becomes a lot harder to understand. Since identities are changing and developing in childhood and adolescence so the trauma just becomes part of that identity. So when it goes, you don't understand who you are and there is nothing to return to because you didn't have a fully developed identity in the first place.

Anyway, most trauma recovery that I've seen and read about focuses on the first aspect and returning to some identity that the survivor had before.

And yet, this doesn't mean that the client cannot experience transformation because recovery from something as negative and awful as trauma, does have the power to be transformational and that's what I want to focus on now.

As a result of as I've mentioned before my trauma recovery meant for the first time in a decade I was pain-free and my trauma and abuse was no longer holding me back. That was a massively scary, hopeful and exciting thing about my life because I could actually start to live my life how I saw fit and I could live my life without the constant fear of beatings and more.

That is very powerful.

Also, trauma recovery allowed me to start building a new identity that is very similar to who I was before. Since I am still someone that loves learning, writing, helping others and trying to save lives in small tiny ways. Like giving blood, being an organ donor and being on the Bone Marrow Register.

Yet in other ways, I am a completely different person. For instance, I now feel like I can date, I am no longer scared of the world and my own family, I know I won't kill myself, I'm pain-free and there is nothing holding me back anymore amongst a whole host of other things.

Therefore, trauma can be very transformational for a client. It converted me from someone who was scared, scarred and traumatised and who was terrified to be who they wanted to be, and made me into someone who loves life, has a social life and is playing around with their new identity.

It's fun and it's exciting.

Of course, I would have liked never had had to go through the trauma in the first place but it all worked out. I'm alive and safe and I am really hopeful and excited about the future because anything could happen now.

I am not trapped in the past, I am not in agony and I want to do things that I never would have done before.

It's exciting.

And that's the point.

As future or current psychologists, we do have the power to help give someone back their life, we have the knowledge and tools to give to someone so they can use it to help them take control of their life back so they can live the life they always wanted to.

It will not be easy for the client at all but it is possible. I am proof of that and so many other amazing clients all over the world have found transformation in their traumatic experiences.

They can rebuild their lives in whatever way they see fit and I think almost every single client will admit to knowing that their life is so much better now after trauma recovery, because they're back in control, and they've shredded the bad aspects of their life away.

It's an interesting thought exercise to think of trauma as a force for good in someone's life, and whilst trauma is bad, the recovery aspect after working through the traumatic event can focus on the positivity, excitement and all the brand-new possibilities that therapy has allowed them to explore.

And that should be very exciting for a client and a therapist, because we are the people that helped our clients realise it for themselves. And that is a wonderful feeling indeed.

IMPORTANCE OF EXPLORING OTHER THERAPIES, EXPLAINING YOURSELF TO A CLIENT AND MORE

After having a bad mental breakdown in August 2023 and then a few smaller ones when the new academic year started I applied for free counselling at the university and when I started it, I was inspired enough to draw a few parrels with other forms of psychotherapy. As well as I want to reflect on the experience so much in a general sense because we can all learn from this.

Especially because this is lived experience that goes beyond our textbooks, lecture theatres and maybe what our lecturers can tell us.

<u>The Importance Of Exploring Therapies</u>

I'll link this to my new therapist in a moment, but something I am starting to discover more and more as I continue to explore psychology is that you need a very playful attitude towards therapy at times. Since I have said time and time again in different psychology places that no one therapeutic model has all the answers for every single client, and all the therapies even the most woo-woo ones can have good elements you can take in case they work with a specific client.

And this playful attitude is flat out not taught at universities and I would almost say that it's discouraged. Since again, I will never ever argue against the Scientist-Practitioner model. Clinical psychologists MUST use science and empirically supported methods of working.

This is why I like Cognitive Behavioural Therapy so much because it is highly effective, there is great research to support it and it is a very accessible therapy.

However, there are other therapies available in the world and for different therapists to use. Also, you might have a client with depression and the vast majority of CBT works great for your client, but there is just something missing or something holding them back from "completing" the therapy and the CBT tricks aren't working for this particular client. That's why having a good knowledge of other therapies is useful because you can borrow tricks and tips from them.

In addition, all the therapeutic models are basically saying the exact same thing in different versions of the same flowery language. You only need to listen or read The Psychology World Podcast "What is Person-Centred Therapy?" episode and the other therapy-based podcast episodes around that time to see the similarities between the cognitive-behavioural approach and the humanistic approaches.

Anyway, my point is that you might learn a lot about CBT in your Masters, but don't limit yourself or your knowledge to that single therapy. Don't limit your knowledge to a single therapy period, whatever it is.

I know you need to keep learning, you'll learn more in the future as you gain experience and if you're in the UK, then you are required to train in at least two therapeutic models to the best of my knowledge.

And instead of seeing this as an exercise in learning about a main therapy and then a minor one that you might use a little but not a lot. Take this learning as an exciting exercise that will allow you to explore mental health more and help improve lives.

The reason why I talk about this is because my therapist uses tons of imagery and metaphors in his therapy work. He mainly focuses on integrative work, and my mind immediately pushed against that (without him knowing) because I wasn't convinced that imagery and metaphor had a place in psychotherapy.

It turns out it does.

And I've learnt a lot about how he works, how he uses metaphor and imagery to help clients and it can be used a lot to help explain concepts or emotional states that are hard to describe with "simple" words. I wrote about it earlier in the day for another book but that will form a chapter after the next reflection because I do believe it is really useful in helping us, current or future, clinical psychologists to understand how this other form of psychotherapy works.

Since imagery and metaphor, in my experience, isn't something you learn about because it can be woo-woo, unempirical and everything else.

This is why at times therapy is as much an art as a science.

The Power Of Explaining Yourself To A Client

Something I always remember from my undergraduate clinical psychology lectures is the importance of explaining yourself to a client before you start therapeutic work. For example, you would explain the limits of confidentiality, the importance of saying "no" if the therapist is wrong, explaining how the therapy will work and just general stuff like that.

That was really interesting to see as a future clinical psychologist, because it was useful to see how to easily and almost carefully he did it. He was careful in the sense that he knew he had to be confident but delicate at the same time because therapy can be overwhelming for a lot of people.

Moreover, as a client myself in that situation, it was a relief to know he wasn't arrogant, he was supportive and he was a great person that I could work with because it was clear he was there to support and work *with* me. Instead of just thinking that he knew stuff and whatnot.

I know from my own learning that therapists are not *meant* to presume they know everything and they are meant to work with the client and everything. But I think everyone still has the fear or what if they don't act like that.

As a result, I just wanted to mention that I know this will seem unimportant, annoying and just a silly little necessity you need to do at the start of working with each client. Yet I can promise you, your future clients will find really useful, really hopeful and it is more powerful than we could ever know from our lectures and textbooks.

This is why listening to real-world lived experience is important and why it is a lot of fun to read or listen to people who have been through things, you hopefully will never have to go through.

MEANING OF THE WORD TRAUMA, DOING IDENTITY WORK WITH CLIENTS AND MORE

As you'll be able to tell from the tone of this reflection, this wasn't necessarily written at first as a clinical psychology reflection as this is a reflection on my first counselling session at my university.

However, I wanted to include it in these pages because it is a massive reflection on my experience of a counselling session, so you will be able to learn from that alone. Yet there are plenty of concepts, explanations of other therapy-based reflections that you'll be able to learn from too. You'll be able to understand and see some of the techniques the counsellor used on me, and what I as a client thought about them.

Of course, nothing in this book is any sort of official advice but you might like an idea and it might be useful for you in your future or current practice. I don't know, but I found this interesting and I think this has the potential to be useful for you whatever stage you are at in your psychology journey.

**

I have to admit that currently as I write this reflection, I'm not entirely sure what book this will be seen in, because my memoir is already written and it's set to be published. Yet if you're reading this then I must have found somewhere to slide this reflection in.

However, I am probably only saying that because I'm procrastinating about doing this reflection. Due to it reflects a larger truth that I lie to myself about constantly, it is the fact that I still need to be careful with my mental health and I still need counselling. Which isn't a bad thing at all and I only feel like this for the various reasons that we'll reflect on throughout this first counselling session.

In addition, just for a bit of context, the counselling was provided for free by my university's mental health support service and the counsellor I was assigned I really like. He gave me a few things to reflect on as an aspiring clinical psychologist, but he was great as a counsellor and I'm looking forward to my sessions with him.

He uses a lot of imagery, metaphor and he does interrupt at times but he only does that for two reasons. One, I expect he's autistic like me so he can't really help it. Two, whenever he does interrupt he only does this to be helpful and useful to me so I really don't mind it.

In terms of context for myself, if you're read my memoir then you've familiar with my pain, trauma and child abuse that I experienced for about a decade. That made me feeling suicidal at times and I self-harmed a fair bit over the years.

Although, after the events and mental breakdown discussed in my memoir and my journey towards healing and trauma recovery, I would never do those things anymore and I'm no longer in pain.

This is important for the context because no longer being in pain, no longer being held back by my trauma and abuse and past made me feel really lost, fragile and my entire world had changed. Since it led to a lot of honest conversations with my family so they now support me.

That's the context for the rest of the reflection and why I wanted counselling, so I knew how to deal with this new reality.

<u>Meaning Of The Word Trauma</u>

One of the first things we looked at in this first counselling session was an interesting take on trauma as a concept, and he wanted me to know the meaning of the word trauma. Then he mentioned how he was giving me this information and I could do with it what I willed. I don't think he really had a specific idea or desire for me to use the knowledge in a certain way.

Then again the entire point of counselling or at least person-centred work is that the client has all the answers, and they just need guidance and encouragement to find the answers for themselves.

Anyway, the word "trauma" comes from the German word "to dream" and we spoke for about a minute about what that could mean. And this was fascinating to me because in clinical psychology, there is an approach called the cognitive approach to mental health. The founding idea of this approach is that it isn't the event themselves that are traumatic or cause us to have negative mental health. It is our interpretation and perception of these events.

For example, if we take social anxiety for a moment that was caused by you getting humiliated at a party leading you to develop an intense fear of parties. It isn't the humiliating part that gave you social anxiety, it is your fear surrounding wanting to make sure that never ever happens again, that's the cause of the social anxiety.

At least in a layman's explanation.

Therefore, when it comes to trauma, it isn't the traumatic event that makes you have all the negative mental health consequences and the maladaptive coping mechanisms. It is how you interpret the events that makes it traumatic.

This helps to explain how two people can go through the exact same event and one can have good mental health and the other doesn't.

Personally, this is useful in a therapy context because it means when it comes to me relating and remembering my trauma of my home environment telling me "you have to beat the gay out of them" and everyone in my wider social support actively hating and wanting to hurt gay people. It means yes, this is extremely traumatic because I heard this constantly for ten years and I was in fear for my life most of the time.

Yet, it wasn't the words and things that were said to me that was traumatic. It was what I reasonably believed the words to mean and the possible consequences.

Of course, this might sound like I'm blaming myself and other trauma survivors but I flat out am not. Instead, I am saying that whenever it comes to a traumatic event humans have a good, survival-based habit of imagining what could happen and what might able if these situations are allowed to repeat.

And that is where a good amount of the negative mental health comes from.

This is why therapy is flat out critical in helping a trauma survivor to move on and help them to move on so they aren't constantly engaging in this extreme imagining.

Identity Changes On Context

One of the reasons why I went to counselling and one of the main aims I have for this round of counselling is that because I am no longer held back by my pain, trauma and abuse I no longer really know who I am.

Since my counsellor likes to use imagery and whatnot I described it to him as a container which is my identity, being filled with water that represents my trauma and then the water being emptied out. Leaving only a few peddles that represents different aspects of my identity, but now there is a lot of empty space and air in the container where I feel I am missing parts of myself with my trauma being dealt with in therapy.

Therefore, I felt really lost before this counselling session because I simply didn't know who I was anymore.

And he didn't say this but this would be too judgemental for a counsellor, but he challenged me on the concept of identity because I now know I was looking at identity wrong.

Which is rather interesting considering I know all this from social psychology research anyway. But identity changes depending on the social group we're in. For example, I engage in a different social identity when I'm at university compared to at home, and when I'm with friends compared to with family, as well as when I'm doing a podcast episode compared to talking with a lecturer.

And so on.

Our social identities are constantly changing and being switched about depending on the context. There is a lot of social psychology research on the topic so if this interests you then definitely check it out.

However, for me in a therapy context, I think what I was looking for was for me to realise that I have a core identity that is *me* and then I have all these different social identities around my Core Self that reflect different aspects of who I am. Yet before, all these different aspects were bound by my pain and trauma and now it isn't there, everything felt disjointed.

I thought I was looking for something to help me out there.

Nonetheless, that wasn't the case because being reminded of such a basic principle in social psychology was really useful for me in figuring out who I am, or at least starting to.

Since at my very core, I am still the same person with or without my trauma. I am a gay person who writes, podcasts, loves their family and I love psychology, writing and transgender stuff (that's a new interest). As well as I am kind, helpful and I always want to keep learning in the areas I am interested in.

That hasn't changed.

And as for the idea that I feel lost because the pain and weight of my past isn't holding me back anymore. That connects with a lot of different things that I will talk about below, but fundamentally, this takes time to learn who I am these days and it is okay to switch social identities.

It is normal and it is critical to functioning in a social world.

Switching social identities doesn't mean I don't know who I am anymore, it is simply me focusing and trying to fit in in a social world.

That's the basic idea and now I'll explain some

other ways how this counselling session helped me with my identity.

Being Reborn and Traveling

Continuing with the idea of metaphor and imagery, at one point in the therapy session, my counsellor started using this weird metaphor for travelling through life events by focusing on nomadic people. Me being me was very unsure on the idea but I turned out loving the idea and it was really interesting.

So we all know that nomadic people move around a lot and they travel from one location that has depleted resources to another area with a plentiful supply of resources.

In addition, nomadic people travel in four stages. Firstly, the nomadic people arrive in a location and they set themselves up comfortably and they basically find themselves and where they fit in that new environment.

Secondly, they get use to that new area, they farm, they work and they live their life in that area.

Thirdly, as resources start to dry up and the environment starts to become less plentiful and useful for the nomadic people, they pack up and they leave the environment that they have called home for so long.

Fourthly, they are travelling and they eventually end up back in a new plentiful environment with new resources. Basically arriving back at stage one again for the cycle to continue.

Now this is useful for exploring and explaining life rolls to people because this is how life works. For example, let's take a fairly basic example of a young person going off to university.

Stage one and two would involve the young person being at home, living their life, going to school and going out with their friends. Then they would start to feel like they need to go to university for self-growth, to improve their career prospects and they might want to take advantage of the university clubbing scene, for instance. This would make them need to pack up their life and travel towards their new destination of university for three years where they need to settle down again, create a new life and live their life at university during their degree.

That sort of idea.

Personally, it is useful to hear him talk about life in this way because he explained how I was in the Fourth Stage and I was traveling. I was traveling from my old life which was defined by pain, trauma and abuse towards my new life where I could be anything I want without pain, trauma and abuse holding me back.

I have no idea where I will end up, who I will become and what social network I will end up with, but I am traveling.

And considering how lost, hopeless and uncertain I felt about everything to do with my identity after my last round of private therapy. It was really useful to have someone tell me that I was traveling and I need to try and enjoy the journey and focus on the fact that this will take time.

Something I struggled with horrifically.

Furthermore, another useful concept he mentioned that helped with my identity crisis was the idea of "being reborn" and this is how I feel to some extent.

At the end of the day, I am not the same person that I was. The old me was filled with self-hate, pain, trauma and they were extremely scared of things not in a pathetic way but they were scared of being discovered and living life how they wanted to.

In addition, the old me had no problem self-harming, wanting to die and they were a "tortured soul" some might say. And they would be right to.

Nonetheless, I am none of those things now and I would never ever commit suicide or self-harm again because I understand it serves no purpose now and it is stupid for me to self-harm because of the faults of others.

As a result, I am a new person that has been reborn to a large extent. As well as there were some interesting connotations that my therapist mentioned during the session, because if you've been reborn then this means that there's a certain level of infancy about you.

For example, you're vulnerable, uncertain and you have a lot of learning to do to understand how the world works similar to how a child has to learn how the physical and social world works.

That is similar to how I feel and I think I agree with the metaphor for the most part. I am an infant in the sense that the new-me has only recently been born and I am very much trying to figure out my place in the world and how this new world works around me considering every single little thing changed for me during my mental breakdown.

It had to and I am glad it did, but I am very unsettled at the moment.

As a result, I am really grateful that he gave me these concepts to focus on and he helped me to understand what everyone else was saying to me about the importance of giving yourself time. Since I now understand using this metaphor that children and infants don't grow over night or over a few weeks, they need to explore the world, test what they like and dislike and slowly build up an identity as they start to understand everything around them.

I do feel a lot, lot better and secure in myself and my identity a few days after the therapy session and I'm looking forward to exploring myself and my new identity as time goes on. I'm even going to start playing Dungeons and Dragons with my friends in the coming weeks, something I never ever thought I would do and I have been known to vow never to play a game like that.

But I am different and it will be fun and interesting for sure.

<u>Transitional Friendships</u>

A final major lesson from this counselling session

was the idea of "transitional friendships" because if you're read my memoir *Healing: A Gay Man's Journey to Happiness, Joy and Recovery From Trauma and Abuse.* Then you'll be familiar with how I lost a dear friend during my mental breakdown because I developed emotional dependency and I basically made that friendship toxic because of my trauma and abuse.

And I do miss them and I have always felt a lot of guilt and uncertainty and pain and… a lot of different emotions for how badly I hurt them and his boyfriend because of everything I went through. But definitely check out my memoir for more information on that and everything else.

Therefore, I spoke to my counsellor about this and he mentioned the normal stuff about it's clear I want to make things right and everything, and they weren't saying I should or shouldn't try to recover this friendship. But they did mention something about transitional friendships.

In other words, this friendship's purpose was to take me from one place and hold my hand until I reached another place and that was the job of the friendship.

This does make perfect sense about the friendship because this friendship did exactly that. It gave me so much support and it forced me to go from my old life of trauma and abuse into my new life. Without this friendship I never would have gone to therapy, have the honest conversations I did with my family and so on.

And I wouldn't have the friends I have now that I met during a social group I joined after starting my trauma recovery.

Therefore, that friendship did take me from one place to another, and I wasn't sure what to make of this idea for ages. But it is helpful to think about this friendship that I murdered because of my pain and abuse and think about it through the lens of there was purpose in it and it did achieve everything it needed to.

It's hard to explain but I did like the idea that transitional friendships exist. As well as whilst I don't know what book this will end up in, I want to mention this concept just in case you find it useful for the future.

Overall, I do enjoy therapy sessions and I love reflecting on them even more because they help me process everything, they help me learn and they help me love my new life and psychology even more.

THE KEY METAPHOR FOR FRIENDSHIPS, IDENTITIES AND WHO WE ARE

Two reflections ago, I mentioned how my current therapist uses a lot of metaphors and imagery in his work and there was a particular metaphor that I really liked and I think this is a really useful metaphor for our future work. I think this is a great metaphor in case you work with autistic people in the future because it can take the abstract concept of friendship and make it more tangible.

And in the words of my therapist, the idea that autistic people cannot engage in imagery and metaphor in the vast, vast majority of cases is "bullshit", so please don't dismiss this automatically.

In addition, I think this metaphor has a lot of potential applications in identity work, definitely with trauma and abuse survivors and I think this could be applied in a thousand more situations if you'll willing to stretch and bend the metaphor enough.

Please enjoy.

**

Following my second therapy session I quickly realised that in the first reflection on my counselling sessions at the university, I didn't mention one of the most useful things I had ever heard. It was a brilliant metaphor that I wanted to focus on more in this reflection because it is really useful and you can expand it and use it in your own friendships.

However, first of all I just wanted to mention that overall I am doing surprisingly well after the last session. I no longer feel lost in who I am, I don't feel like the my identity is empty and shattered because I no longer have the abuse and pain and trauma holding me back. As well as what I am most interested in is some of my resilience is coming back.

All trauma and abuse survivors are naturally highly resilient because you just have to be to survive, but when my pain and everything was dealt with. I didn't need to be resilient anymore or I didn't know how to be resilient anymore. Thankfully, my natural resilience is starting to return which is a wonderful feeling.

Also, I am just starting to learn a lot more about friendships, who I am and my identity in general. Mainly, because I'm playing around with small changes to my look, some really, really subtle feminine changes. Like I brought myself a small rose gold bracelet that I wore to Trans group and then to a university social this week.

No one noticed and no one cared.

So I am slowly growing and learning who I am nowadays. As well as it is great to have finally realised that this identity work is just a learning process and it will take time, and that isn't a bad thing.

That's the overview of how I'm doing, the realisations since the last counselling session and everything else in general.

Now let's move onto the metaphor.

<u>The Key Metaphor</u>

I mentioned before that my therapist really likes to draw on metaphors and imagery in their therapeutic work with clients. And towards the end of last session, he was talking about imagine you're in a house and someone who you haven't met before comes up to your house (which represents you and your life) and you both start talking.

If you feel a connection and want to become friends with them then you might give them a key to your porch area, so you invite them into your life a little more.

If you don't like them or if a friendship doesn't develop then you don't give them a key at all. Since they're staying outside your life and they don't deserve to come in.

Then overtime as the friendship develops, you might start giving them more and more keys so they can come deeper into your life and they can be taken to different rooms that represent or are metaphors for different things. For example, if you'll willing to give your friend a key to the living room then this might represent for you (these are always what these rooms mean for you) that you're comfortable around them to socialise and entertain them. But you might not give them a key to the kitchen (the heart of the home where some of the most important functions happen perhaps) or your bedroom or another private, personal space.

Overall, so far, the metaphor is really useful in understanding how friendships work in the sense that there are different levels to friendships, and friends take time to evolve and grow so you gain enough trust and consent in the relationship to move through each other's lives or houses.

In addition, this doesn't have to be a real house or based on one, because you can add as many rooms as you like that represent different aspects of yourself. This is important for something I'll mention later on.

For example, in the session, because I used to be really into Warhammer 40,000 and now I'm going to be starting Dungeons and Dragons in a few weeks, because my friends are playing. We added a gaming room to my house and this was important, because let's face it, there is a good level of vulnerability to your gaming room (if you have one). You tend to act silly, authentically and without a care for what other people think of you as long as you're all having fun when playing a game. Especially a wargame like Warhammer or a roleplaying game like D&D.

Therefore, if I'm willing to give someone a key to

the gaming room then this helps me to understand that I am close with this friend. And that's a good thing.

Over To You

Before I explicitly focus on why I find this metaphor so useful and how I use this in my everyday life (I've used it a lot over the past week), I want to say that in your own metaphorical houses you can add any rooms that you want, as well as you can decorate them however you want.

For example, one thing we did in the session was we focused on my bedroom, because I was stressing that was a very, very personal space where I slept, it was where I had had breakdowns and a lot of my mental health was tied up in that room.

As a result, he got me to describe this room in detail and thankfully, my real bedroom reflects who I am and how I feel currently very well, so I just described my real bedroom. Therefore, because I'm feeling good it's very well-lit with beautiful photo artwork on the walls that adds beauty and nature to the bedroom, as well as my bedroom is practical but it is spacious and airy and it doesn't feel negative or depressive.

That imagery reflects who I am with my subtle interest in beautiful real artwork that are photos, I focus on being practical or I want my spaces to feel positive because I am a positive person.

On the flip side, when I'm down or when the Gay part of me was being abused, traumatised and wanted to die. I invoke the imagery of a scared 16-year-old boy in a very dark bedroom terrified of what was going to happen next and if it was going to get beaten or killed.

That simple piece of imagery explains a lot about my feelings and thoughts when it comes to trauma and abuse.

To bring this back to you, if you want to make this imagery or metaphor in therapy then do it but make sure you customise the imagery to how you feel. It might take some practice but if you're finding it hard to describe what you're going through, imagery is great to fall back on.

Furthermore, when it comes to your own rooms, you can create whatever rooms you want. For example, if you seriously love gardening then have a massive garden. Yet if there is a section of your garden that contains your most prized plants or a bunch of garden toys for the kids or something then maybe have a metaphorical fence around that stuff. Since you might sit outside for a coffee with a friend you like but don't love. Yet you might only show your best friend, your most prized plants.

I don't know but you need to use the metaphor as you see fit representing the important aspects of yourself that are personal and who represent you.

This includes rooms that you might not show anyone besides from yourself or even a romantic partner that you're committed to for the long term. For instance, I'm not really sure how many secrets I have these days but there are things, certain opinions and other interests that I wouldn't just share with anyone. Some of these opinions I might keep to myself period and these might be represented by small rooms with doors covered in shadows on a floor with a staircase that only I have the key to.

It's just an idea.

Then finally for the theory or setting up the metaphor, this is a great metaphor for understanding that certain friendships belong in certain places, and certain friendships function in some domains but not others.

The example we used in the therapy session was how the garage of a house is where you tend to be practical, make things and be resourceful. So you would only want practical friends in there that are good with their hands, so you might not want some other people in the garage. For instance, I would want some of my old scouting friends in the garage because they're good with their hands and they are good at creating things and that's a fun activity. But I wouldn't always allow the same people into my living room because I don't want to socialise and entertain them outside the garage.

Some more general examples include, I'm a Student Ambassador at my university and I have a few friends from that domain of my life. Meaning it is normal to see them in my Outreach room, but it would be wrong to see them in my living room or bedroom. Those friends don't belong there. It doesn't mean they aren't my friends, it just means they don't belong there.

Equally, if my university friends come into my writing room or something that would be wrong too, because my university friends aren't my work or writing friends. They flat out don't belong in this area of my life.

Therefore, in a way, I guess this helps me to understand that friendships can be limited to a certain area of your life and that's okay. There's nothing wrong with that and I think that is healthy too. You need your own space and you don't want your friends to dominate every aspect of your life.

That's enough of the theory side for now so let me explain how I use this metaphor in practice.

How I Use The Metaphor In Practice?

Overall, I really like this metaphor because it allows you to check in with friendships, see how they're developing and generally, they allow me to understand that I'm making more progress than I thought.

For example, over the past week I've spent a lot of time thinking about friendships, talking to friends and going out with them and I've realised that the definition of friend is a lot looser than I imagined.

This is a good thing.

Since I used to believe that a friend was only a person who I had a really close bond with. That is still true but there are other shades or flavours or types of friendships that are different but still no less valuable.

For example, I was at Trans group Wednesday night and I spent a good two(ish) hours talking to a trans man friend that I hadn't really spoken too much, because they had bad mental health before and listening to their experiences caused me to have a breakdown later that night.

Yet it was great to talk to him and it was fun and it was just nice.

Later on I had a conversation with another friend for about 30 minutes, and it was the first time we had probably spoken just the two of us but it was fun. I learnt exactly how much I don't understand or know about D&D but she's going to help me create a character idea.

And yes, I still have no idea what that means.

So anyway, I was back at my great aunt's that night because I was staying with her after taking my Grandad there after his eye operation. And I was laying in bed and I just realised that I am starting to build a good little group of friends because the trans man and trans woman I was talking to I would happily give them the keys to my living room.

Then there's another person I talk to weekly who these two people are great friends with, and I would give them keys to my Gaming Room and a whole bunch of other spaces too that these two people don't have access to.

For now.

Therefore, I like how this metaphor can be stretched and adapted for whatever you need. The house can be added to more and more to reflect the rooms and spaces and aspects of yourself that you need.

Overall, this is a metaphor that I use to evaluate and monitor friendships and it helps me as a survivor and an autistic person to understand how complex friendships are in a way that is easy to understand. Because I can see it and this metaphor helps make the complex nature of friendships more tangible and real.

My unofficial advice for you if you're trying to work out who you are and anything to do with friendships would be to give about your own house and then see where you would allow your different friends to go within that house.

And a final tip I learnt from this session, it is perfectly okay and normal for friends not to have access to all the rooms. We always have aspects of ourselves that hide and change depending on the person. We probably need to hide certain aspects of ourselves otherwise we would be extremely vulnerable if we were completely, completely open without a single secret to other people.

So it's okay if you don't let anyone besides yourself into certain rooms.

Because that's healthy.

THE STUPIDITY OF OUT OF AREA PLACEMENTS

Something I am seriously known for amongst the long term readers of these clinical psychology reflections is that I am a famously bad reader of The Psychologist by the British Psychological Society. I have issues of the magazine that I got over 14 months ago and still haven't read, so that's why I enjoy these reflections because it makes me actually read the magazine. Since every so often I get a very interesting idea for a reflection.

This is one of those times.

Interestingly enough, a few days before I read this article, my mother actually mentioned to me that one of her friend's wife's (who's a clinical psychologist) mentioned how in England the county of your birth has to pay for your mental health care. Whilst I have no idea if this is true, I have a good sense that it is.

As a result, when a person needs psychological

support, one of three things happen. A person who is struggling with mental health support is treated in their local area where they live, they are returned to their birth county for treatment or they are sent somewhere out of their local area because there's room there.

Of course, the UK Government pledged to ban Out of Area placements for people receiving mental health treatments in March 2021. Yet as everyone in the UK knows, this current UK Government lies about everything so since March 2021 (the proposed month this was to be scrapped), another 209,000 people have received Out of Area placements.

That figure came from an article in the July/August 2022 issue of the Psychologist. That means in basically a year and a quarter 209,000 people have been ripped away from their social support networks and everything they knew just because of the stupidity of this idea and scheme.

That number has most probably doubled at the time of writing this reflection.

Therefore, for the rest of this reflection, I want to reflect on why *I* think this is stupid but to be a little balanced, I'll reflect on the possible reasons behind this scheme. Then I'll propose ways to fix these reasons.

Why I Think Out Of Area Placements Are Stupid?

We know from a lot of different research studies that social support, friends and family are critical for our mental health. For example, a person who has a lot of friends and family members with good, high-quality relationships with them is less likely to have mental health difficulties than people with fewer connections and experience loneliness.

We can all agree on that.

Also, for certain mental health conditions and for certain people, routine, structure and being in a familiar environment is important. As well as I would ever say that whenever everyone is going through hell and experiencing clinically significant levels of distress, we want to be somewhere we know and are familiar with.

Therefore, this is where the stupidity of Out of Area placements lie because we are taking people with mental health difficulties, hundreds of miles away to a brand-new city, town or hospital, whatever to receive treatment. They won't be able to see their friends, their family, their entire lives will be disrupted.

That will only add to their distress and the distress of their families and friends.

Since no one gets an NHS appointment these days unless the situation is dire. I know to get access to psychological treatment in Child and Adolescent Mental Health Services (CAMHS) a child needs to do two *believable* suicide attempts. And even adult services because they are so underfunded and stretched, if a person gets an appointment, it is only because they're been on a waiting list for years or they are so "bad" or so distressed that they need to jump the queue for lack of a better term.

As a result, the people who get NHS appointments are extremely, extremely distressed to the point of self-harm, suicide or a number of other "risky" mental health difficulties. So the very notion of that we want to add to their psychological distress by taking them away from their friends, family and routine is beyond stupid.

Let me add a personal example that really explains why this would be beyond stupid for someone like me.

Why This Would Be Dire For Me?

I mentioned before that in August 2023 I had a major mental breakdown because of years of trauma and abuse that led me to self-harm and there were even some thoughts of suicide but no real plan and definitely no attempt. Let's say by some fantasy miracle that I got an NHS appointment when I needed it. That's funny to think that might happen.

Then that's say the NHS wanted to send me to Cornwall or Cumbria (two counties on opposite ends of the country and at least 4 hours away from my home) because those Trusts have some space in their mental health services for me.

Well, I can promise you, the very idea of my routines, being away from my family and friends and being away from what little normality I had left. That would not have helped whatsoever and that would have made me worse.

It was actually the tiny things that really helped me during my breakdown. I could still write, I could still do online classes and the associated assignments, I could read and I could do some small things when I was feeling like I was dying inside.

If I couldn't write, watch my online courses or read or just do anything that I loved to do because I was in a strange, new environment. That would have been even worse for me.

Therefore, as annoyed as I am at the NHS, no actually the government for crippling the NHS so much that mental health services in the UK are next to useless unless you have tried to kill yourself. I am glad I barely managed to deal with everything alone, I burnt my life down in the process, but I managed to stay alive.

I managed that but if I had been sent to an Out of Area placement then I doubt the results would have been the same. And I fairly sure I would have been retraumatised because I just wouldn't have that sense of routine, structure and safety that I depended on during my breakdown.

I would have been surrounded by strangers, new medical things in a hospital or wherever people end up and I would have hated it.

I would hardly be the only one.

Possible Reasons For Out Of Area Placements And Their Possible Solutions

To be honest I think Out of Area placements really come down to funding and capacity issues and the solution is the same.

The lack of funding in the NHS and its mental

health services means that different NHS Trusts have to decide how serious someone has to be before they are seen too because it is flat out impossible to see and treat everyone with mental health difficulties.

Also, there is limited funding available so if a Trust can transfer over to another NHS Trust so this other Trust has to spend money then I think all NHS Trusts would prefer that option. Especially as the NHS Trusts are run like businesses like public sector healthcare settings.

On the whole, the solution is simple (they say smiling) there has to be more funding for mental health services so the NHS Trusts can expand their services and keep people inside their local areas where they still have contact with their friends and family members and hopefully their normal lives.

But I know the UK Government always bangs on about funding and yet we need "real funding". We need the funding and extra money from central government to go to the services themselves instead of being used on Managers and all the other stupid ways that money in the NHS is wasted by the people at the top.

That is definitely an interesting area you might want to look at in your own time. It's called Managerialism in the NHS in case you're interested.

And I was listening to a podcast yesterday at the time of writing and this woman (who was yet another victim of US gun violence) and she was explaining how her medical bills might come to $200,000 at the end of her treatment and she was curious about how her money would be used.

Would the great nurses and specialists that treated her use it? Or would it be used to line the pockets of other higher up people that didn't help her much?

It is a good question for healthcare systems around the world but that is beyond the scope of this reflection.

Overall, Out of Area Placements are stupid in my personal opinion because they mean taking people with severe mental health difficulties away from their normal lives, their friends and their family members that offer them love and support, and stick them in a strange new environment that only adds to their distress.

This shouldn't happen and things can be changed to make sure this doesn't happen, but it requires solving a lot of problems that I doubt the government and the highest tiers of the NHS are interested in solving.

ARE ALL BARRIERS IN CLINICAL PSYCHOLOGY THE SAME HEIGHT?

When I was flicking through the December 2022 edition of The Psychologist Magazine, there was this article from a man talking about him feeling out of place and almost like an imposter on the UK's NHS "Aspiring Clinical Psychologist" scheme.

It's a scheme designed to help people who cannot undertake a Masters nor undertake unpaid work experience to get work experience and a partial education towards becoming a fully qualified psychologist.

In the article, the man was talking about how much of a fraud he felt because he was white, wasn't from an ethnic minority and he didn't have any other characteristics that would disadvantage him. The only reason he was on the scheme was because he was from a poor background so he couldn't undertake unpaid work experience or do a Masters degree.

And then the article went on to talk about how

he realise he did belong on the scheme but it still made him think about his own privileges and that not all the barriers in clinical psychology are the same height. The barriers to the profession were a lot lower for him compared to a black person from a poor background.

Personally, this got me thinking about my own privileges and disadvantages, but firstly I want to mention that this man might have been white and he didn't have any other disadvantages besides the fact that he was from a poor background. He still 100% deserved to be on this scheme because he met the criteria, he needed the help and it benefited all the future clients he was going to see.

He was suffering from self-doubt and imposter syndrome, which is understandable, but he shouldn't have felt that way about himself.

Furthermore, I think the reason why this really got me thinking is because of my own appearance, status and disadvantages. Since I am a white male from a middle class family in a poor area. Those are my advantages and those have been very useful to me in my life.

Also, I am gay but you would never know from looking at me so I can hide that part of myself very well if needed. As well as I am part of the trans community as a non-binary person but again, you would never be able to tell.

Then finally, I have suffered really bad mental health and I had tons of lived experience of mental health difficulties behind me. You would think that would certainly be an advantage in clinical psychology and it very much can be, but people are still weary. And there are still unconscious biases at play during the recruitment process, even within clinical psychology.

Yet again, you would never know I have had horrific mental health in the past, because I hide it very well.

Therefore, what got me thinking about this article was that I definitely know how this man feels. Since there have been times I have wanted to apply for minority-focused bursaries, opportunities and more but I have stopped myself because I don't *feel* disadvantaged at times.

Of course, I am perfectly aware that I am disadvantaged and there have been times when people in positions of power have made that perfectly clear to me in very non-subtle ways.

However, I keep telling myself the same lie over and over again about how I don't need these things. Even though it would have helped me, my future and my career if I had applied for these things a few years ago.

It's interesting that I try to convince myself that I am perfectly okay even now, but I am not because I am disadvantaged and I shouldn't be scared to recognise it.

On the whole, when it comes to myself, in the future if there is an opportunity that comes up for minorities. Then I need to be more open and honest with myself about looking into it and allowing myself to apply if I think I meet the criteria.

For everyone else reading this, if there is an opportunity that you meet the criteria for, whether it's aimed at minorities or not, you should go for it. Getting a job in psychology is hard enough for all of us, but it is even harder for other people that face more barriers than most.

Look for opportunities, exploit them and help yourself to build a Resume or the career that you want.

Don't let self-doubt, imposter syndrome or anything else hold you back.

IN VULNERABLE TIMES WE REMEMBER WHAT OTHERS SAY

Sometimes when it comes to the Psychologist magazine, it's the content that gets me interested, sometimes it is very much the writer (like the amazing Lucy Johnstone) but other times it is simply the title that gives me something to reflect on.

Therefore, in one of the late 2022 issues, there was an article titled the same as the name of this reflection, and whilst I didn't really read the article itself because I didn't find it too interesting. I still really liked the title.

Since it is very true and I think we can reflect on this both personally as well as professionally.

<u>The Personal Perspective</u>

When it comes to being vulnerable, I think there are two main types that we can focus on here, psychological distress during a mental health crisis, or the being vulnerable outside of a crisis.

What I mean by being vulnerable outside of a

crisis, this might be what happens during a breakup, the loss of a loved one and generally when you feel really vulnerable and you want other people to support you.

This is a time when we remember who was there for us, who made us feel good and who made us feel safe in amongst the chaos of everything that happened. I remember when my Nan died a few months and my mother received a lot of great support from her friends even though their relationship was both dead and extremely complex.

In that time of emotional uncertainty where my mother was processing her feelings for that awful woman, she remembered and loved her friends and family for supporting her despite the logical reaction to be nothing. But she did have an emotional reaction because she still lost her mother physically.

Anyway, whenever we have a friend or family member going through stuff, it is important to remember to support them, be there for them and just check in. I don't believe for a moment it has to be very grand or important, it can simply be a check-in.

They will remember that simple gesture of kindness when everything has passed, and it will pass in the end. That applies just as much as to you as it does to your friends and family members.

On the flip side, if you, your friends or family members are having a mental health crisis then they will certainly remember who was there for them and who wasn't.

I remember a lot of what my friend said to before just before the worse my breakdown. I remember what my therapist said when I was trying to rebuild my life and I remember a fair amount of the kind, supportive words that my parents said when they finally decided to take my mental health seriously and actually support me.

I'll always remember and appreciate them all for that, and it helps to remind me that I am loved, supported and appreciated. And me and my parents are now a lot closer after those honest conversations and I really do remember what we said and how I felt during that time.

Overall, when it comes to vulnerable times, it is perfectly okay to experience these feelings because they are natural and a result of something bad that happened. It is okay to lean on people to support you and it is okay to be annoyed at people that don't say things to you, and it is even better if you remember the people that were great and kind to you.

You might be surprised where the sources of support come from.

I know I was.

The Professional Perspective

When it comes to clinical psychology and being a future or current therapist, we see amazing people that are having very vulnerable times and moments, they're experiencing clinically significant levels of distress and they're dealing with a lot of mental health difficulties.

Therefore, like I have mentioned millions of times before on the podcast and in these reflections, what a therapist says matters. Yet it isn't only *what* they say, it is how they say it, how they interrupt or don't and how they make a client feel.

As a result, we really can expand the title of this reflection at its heart because what a psychologist does *with* a client during difficult times matters a lot. Psychologists have the power to help them, to support them and help to feel better for the first time in ages.

However, in the very rare event that a psychologist isn't great, if we say something dismissive, cold or we misunderstand something to an extreme degree then a client will remember this. They will probably remember the negative of what was said, of how bad they felt afterwards and they will probably find it helpful.

Of course, most of the time this won't happen because being compassionate, knowing how to talk to clients and how to think about responding to clients will be covered in your training and you will improve with experience.

That's why something I learnt from my counselling sessions from a clinical psychology perspective is it's okay to take an extra few moments to think about responding to a client. It's better to spend an extra five seconds thinking about a good way to phrase it than to say something completely unhelpful.

And I also learnt from my counselling session that if you say something that might be pushed back against by the client because they might see it as unhelpful. Then you might want to say something along the lines of "I want to gently challenge that idea and you can push back if you want" in a careful tone.

When he said that to me, it was useful in understanding that I was an equal in the therapy session and what he was doing was out of respect and he wanted to help me.

See, it's been a few days since that session but I still remember it.

Overall, when it comes to clinical psychology being able to be respectful, sensitive and aware of our client's thoughts, feelings and behaviours are really important when it comes to helping them through vulnerable times because they will remember what was said.

Words have the power to change lives for the good and for the bad. Training helps us know a lot about how to talk to clients but it is us that speaks the words at the end of the day.

So we have to be aware, not scared, not nervous or overly concerned, but just aware that our words have power and our clients will remember what we say, we do and how we make them feel.

WHAT'S MISSING FROM MENTAL HEALTH CAMPIGIANS?

Something I think is great about the past few years, and especially the COVID-19 pandemic, is that mental health campaigns have become really important, easy-to-see and they have received a lot of support.

As an aspiring clinical psychologist myself, I am really happy to see that mental health (at least in the public eye) is finally getting the recognition and attention it deserves. Granted, in the mental health settings and different levels of government it is still not being treated as seriously as physical health but that's a topic for another time.

However, in the September 2022 edition of The Psychologist, there was an interesting focus and spread on the idea that mental health campaigns in their current state aren't actually that great. Due to they're effective at reducing the stigma and helping to raise awareness for how common various mental health difficulties are, but they are still missing a critical piece of the puzzle.

They don't motivate people to get professional help.

I'm very much in two different minds about this article, because I think it is largely true. I will never argue that mental health campaigns are not effective at making mental health conditions known, and laypeople are starting to understand how common they are and their negative side effects.

There are so many I cannot really focus on just one but I think Pringles did a good advert a while back about just asking and focusing on how someone *actually* is. It's a great advert considering in the UK the question of "how are you?" is the biggest waste of time ever. The response is always the same and it is always a lie, everyone says "they're good thanks," without thinking about it even if their life is terrible.

It is just a cultural factor.

Nonetheless, that sort of preventative mental health advert definitely has its place in the world, because it is useful to give people tips and tricks to help the people around them with their mental health before it develops into a "full-blown" mental health difficulty that causes clinically significant levels of distress.

Then another type of mental health advert I see a lot is the focus on statistics and facts that highlight how common different conditions are. Again, these are badly needed to help normalise and reinforce the idea that it is okay to talk about mental health and get help.

And there lies the factor that is missing from mental health campaigns and it is only now after reflecting on the different campaigns that I've seen, I realised how true this factor is.

There is no real focus on getting professional help and dealing with the mental health difficulties surrounding that aspect.

I've spoken in my memoir, on the podcast and probably in these clinical psychology reflections that going to see a therapist and getting professional help is scary as hell. It takes so much courage, so much determination and so much fear that it stops a lot of people.

And that's before we consider the stupid myths surrounding mental health that society has created.

Therefore, I really do agree that I think we have reached a point where the "commonality" and "preventative" types of adverts should take a backseat for a while. We still need them to be about and people still need them, but I think we now need to move towards campaigns and adverts that deal with getting professional help.

It is all well and good us telling people that 50% of people get depression in their life time (I just made up that number by the way) if we don't tell them what to do next and we help them gather up the courage to seek professional help.

I firmly, firmly believe that people will only get

professional help when they are ready but I know from personal experience, it only takes one push in the right direction from people to help a client get on the therapeutic journey towards changing their life for the better.

And if we could develop an advert or campaign that helps inspire that change or the start of the client's journey then that is going to be immensely, immensely powerful and we could help a lot of people.

Advertising definitely works for products and services, so let's turn our attention towards helping people help themselves to improve their lives.

So they can experience less psychological distress, less emotional pain and less maladaptive coping mechanisms. Let's help give them their lives back.

BE SURE NOT TO INTELLECTUALLY GASLIGHT SOMEONE?

One other article I want to reflect on from the September 2023 issue of The Psychologist is a great article focusing on intellectually gaslighting the public and someone by saying that the only threats to humans were from the natural world. Granted, the article was slotted into another series of articles focused on COVID-19 but the article was still wrong.

Therefore, because this article has a lot to do with mental health, the NHS and clinical psychology as a whole, I will certainly be reflecting on it in these pages.

However, just for the sake of clarifying, below is a definition of Gaslighting taken from an episode of The Psychology World Podcast.

"Gaslighting is a form of emotional abuse where someone uses psychological manipulations to cause another person to question their reality. It can happen between two people in any relationship. Like friendships, working relationships and romantic relationships. The gaslighter preserves their own sense of self and power over the other person who ends up adopting the gaslighter's version of reality over their own.

The reason why we need to look at this is because it's important to distinguish gaslighting from normal and healthy behaviours. Like disagreeing and we need to understand when a conflict turns into gaslighting."

In the article, the author proposed that the only serious threats to humanity would come from the natural world in the form of diseases that was the general jist of the article. Then something I rather like about The Psychologist in more recent issues is they publish criticisms and responses to previous articles and the response to this really got me thinking.

Since I completely disagree that the natural world will produce the most serious threats to humans in terms of health, mental health and basically everything else.

I will not lie. COVID-19 and other pandemics are beyond horrific and they sadly kill millions of people, but these are thankfully rare and considering what humans do to themselves in terms of mental health, the natural world cannot hold a candle to us.

For example, as all of you know, I live in the UK and this is not a good country to live in. It is better than other countries for sure, but in recent times, we are experiencing cost of living crisis that is worse compared to the USA and most EU countries, many people are struggling to pay their bills, many people are having to go to food banks just to survive, there is a mental health crisis in the country and we have a free (at the time of writing) health service that has been degraded so badly by the UK Government that my healthcare system is always strained and close to breaking point.

And that's all before we talk about the climate crisis and how human activity is making that worse than it ever would have been without human involvement.

Also, war's a massive human factor that is upending lives, causing mass migration of refugees and war causes a lot of negative mental health outcomes for those affected and Post-Traumatic-stress disorder.

Furthermore, we have a government that is trying to restrict legal protections for minority groups, waging a culture war on trans people, reducing our Right To Protest and actively arresting people who *might* protest and *might* make a disruptive protest.

That isn't how democracy works but that is certainly beyond the scope of this book, as well as I have reflected on these disgusting laws in previous volumes.

In addition, there are plenty of other facets of everyday life that are not ideal and have gotten worse over recent years according to research and so far, I have just rehashed what the response to the article said in The Psychologist.

However, notice how all of those problems come from human activity and human political decisions.

As a result, I firmly believe that to say that the natural world is the only source of threats and dangers to humanity, is stupid at its best and downright gaslighting at its worst. Since if you ask any British person then they will say that the UK Government is useless and it is destroying the healthcare system that so many of us rely amongst their many other faults.

So for a leading psychologist to say in this article that human factors, political factors and the decisions taken by governments aren't important and doesn't cause 99% of these real-world problems that are impacting the mental health and lives of innocent people, is gaslighting I think.

We all know that if governments made different decisions that supported the most vulnerable, supported us and were based on research then the problems might not go away entirely. Yet the psychological distress they caused would be lessened.

One such example would be if the UK Government listened to psychologists and other healthcare professionals about what needs to happen to fix the NHS. They need to restructure it were there is less managerialism, mental health is taken more seriously and the NHS has real funding so we can actually reduce some of these waiting times.

It will never happen and I do suspect the UK

Government wants the NHS to collapse so the US health insurance companies (that donate massive sums of money to their party each year) can come in and expand into the UK market. You really should read into that if you're interested.

Anyway, the media has covered these stories, politicians have called each other out for causing these problems and at the heart of it regardless of your political orientation, we know that political decisions have the power to negatively impact the mental health and lives of innocent people.

So to say that this doesn't happen is gaslighting and very cruel.

Thankfully, all of these can be reversed in time, but not by politicians to be honest because they don't tend to change their minds once they're made a decision that harms people. The past three UK Prime Ministers have proven that beyond reasonable doubt (and for our international audience I'm talking about the 3 Prime Ministers we had in a single year in 2022).

Instead I think the change and hopeful improvement for the lives of innocent people, that will have a knock-on effect for their mental health and us as future or current clinical psychologists, will perhaps come from a new UK Government but I sort of doubt it.

Instead I think as psychologists and psychology organisations continue to battle for recognition and different policy changes, I think over time (and I'm being negative here and I am going to say years and years) psychology, research and an understanding of the importance of mental health will become more important.

Therefore, the impact on mental health of political decisions and human activity might be given a little more weight in the future.

On the whole, the entire point of this reflection was to show you that intellectual gaslighting is a thing and you shouldn't do it. Whenever you make a psychological claim, make sure it is real and you aren't gaslighting people that know the truth, because human activity and the decisions made by others that impact other people's lives are massive threats to our mental health and they happen a lot more frequently than pandemics and other threats from the natural world do.

Finally, this is why I am a massive believer in the therapeutic principles of our client is the expert in themselves, they know themselves best and we can challenge them and their beliefs of course but we should never dismiss them. What they believe is valid, and it might be biased, reflective of a faulty thinking pattern or something else entirely but it should always be believed.

Don't gaslight your clients just because you think you know what's best and you think you know what happened to them in their life even though you have never met them before.

HOW DO WE MAKE PSYCHOLOGY RESEARCH MATTER?

The vast, vast majority of people reading this book have done at least a psychology undergraduate degree, if not a Masters in clinical psychology, so we are all well aware of the importance and how to do psychology research.

However, psychology research is all well and good but there is still the critical problem all research faces, we need to understand how to make the psychology research matter to the general public, policy makers and other stakeholders so the research can have a real-world impact.

This was the focus of an article in The Psychologist in March 2023 and I want to reflect on it, because it is flat out critical. Since one of the many reasons why I love psychology is because it is useful, it can save lives and it can give people such hope in their darkest moments, at least clinical psychology can do that. Yet all the other subdisciplines of psychology have their own "superpowers" too.

However, it is great psychology can do all those things but that only happens if the people in charge of these services, in government and the general public can understand, appreciate and apply these psychology findings.

And academic psychology does not help itself at all.

As a result of psychology research is done by academics, which are people that focus on academic writing because this is required to get it academically published in a good journal, so they can advance their careers. Academics have never ever been trained in how to make their research accessible for the masses and most of them have no idea at all how they would go about explaining their research to the general public.

This is certainly a massive problem within academia, because it is a massive bubble that is almost an echo chamber. They create and do their research for each other and their precious journals. Even though if you talk to them, they will almost always say they do research so they can have a real-world impact.

And there lies the disconnect between academia and the real-world. The real-world is run by non-psychology people that don't really understand research, academic writing and they have their own agendas. This means you cannot approach them or talk to them like fellow academics, if you want them to listen to you and take you seriously and even take your ideas onboard, then you have to talk to them like a real person.

As well as play up to their egos, their ambitions and what makes them look good. It is simply how those in power work.

In addition, this has been spoken about a lot in clinical psychology over the years. The academic researchers work away on clinical psychology topics finding out useful things for clinical psychologists to use with clients, and then they write up their pretty little reports without any regard for any useful or practical advice or steps for how this can be used in the real world to improve lives.

As you can probably tell I am really annoyed by this disconnect, but it is how academia works.

Academia and academics aren't always based in reality and the real-world. I am not trying to disrespect academics because they are lovely people if not a little too passionate at times about their research. Almost to the point where everything else in life becomes lesser than their passion for their research.

Anway, I am highlighting this problem because if psychology academics ever want to have a real impact in the world then they need to help make this more accessible to non-psychology people.

I know a lot of people are trying to do this in different ways. For example, it is why I write my books and I host The Psychology World Podcast, it is me breaking down psychology topics into easy-to-understand episodes. It is still aimed at psychology students and professionals but it is written in a way that makes it easy to understand in case anyone else finds it too.

Furthermore, this is why with my current mental health research on the gender-affirming clothing on transgender youth, I'm trying to make it useful in both the academic and practical sense. I'll be including recommendations and practical findings for mental health practitioners and those working with transgender youth when I write up the academic paper in the vain hope of publishing it in a journal.

If not, I'll transfer the knowledge and the findings into a book so it is still available for people to learn from. As well as I will convert some of it to a podcast episode so the practical stuff is available for free to people who might benefit from it.

Of course, I know I am only able to do these things because of my amazing readers and podcast listeners (thank you by the way), but I guess this is me trying to fight the good fight and help make psychology research matter. So I can share this knowledge and show and prove to non-psychology people that psychology research can improve lives, be useful and help decrease psychological distress.

Yet if no one writes about this in an accessible, engaging and interesting way then people will never know the power of psychology research and nothing will change in the world.

That is sad, tragic and something that has to

change in academia, so if you want to go into academia then please, bear this reflection in mind. It might help you make more of an impact than you ever thought possible.

WHAT DO YOU WANT TO BE KNOWN FOR ON SOCIAL MEDIA?

Of all the different inspirations and articles and real world things that get me thinking and reflecting, I have to admit that this idea from the October 2023 issue of The Psychologist Magazine might be an outlier of sorts. Since there was an article that was talking about digital legacies and wanting to be known for something on social media long after we're gone.

I think this is a logical next extension of legacies because currently and in the past, everyone has been so focused on *doing* or creating or building something to form their legacies. For example, we know Van Gogh, Picasso and Da Vinci because they created stunning art amongst other things as part of their legacy. As well as I am sure in your own country there are famous examples of people that have done great things and built impressive features of a country. One example that comes to mind is Effiel who created the Effiel Tower in Paris.

Anyway, I believe that as we continue to move into the digital world, there will be a growing emphasis on digital legacies.

All of these ideas and drives behind creating a legacy will have clinical psychology and mental health implications. You only need to read my book _Social Media Psychology_ to understand the positive and negatives of social media on mental health.

Therefore, I want to reflect on this idea for future and current clinical psychologists, because one of the aims of the profession is to help us impart our knowledge to the next generation of psychologists. This is why in an ideal world clinical psychologists split their time between working in clinical practice and teaching at universities, but the time constraints and work pressures make that balance impossible.

As a result, social media is another good avenue for clinical psychologists, and us students once we have qualified, to share information. And to be honest, of course non-qualified people cannot call themselves clinical psychologists, they can still help share knowledge, insights and inspirations to people across the world.

That is the beauty of social media.

If we take myself as an example, I host The Psychology World Podcast every Monday without fail and in each episode, I talk about psychology news, a personal update that touches on university or my own psychology experience briefly and then a main psychology topic.

Then on a Monday this goes out to YouTube and all major podcast apps allowing people around the world to listen and learn about psychology. As well as I share the podcast episode on Twitter, Facebook and LinkedIn and Pinterest.

Therefore, I tend to use social media as a way of sharing knowledge, getting engagement and helping people learn more about psychology. Of course, I sometimes do this a little half-ass considering I used to be a lot more active on Twitter before He took it over and ruined the platform. But I do try to be a person people interested in psychology can come to so they can learn interesting things.

There is a larger point I want to make in a moment.

In addition, in terms of me as a fiction author, on Facebook and Instagram, I always try to share a book recommendation, something interesting about me, a Weird Word Wednesday thing and a film or TV recommendations. I do this because I want my fiction author accounts to be entertaining, interesting and a place where people can come to to get good recommendations.

I want to be remembered as an entertainer, a storyteller and a person that makes people smile and find interesting.

Therefore, I cater and craft my social media accounts accordingly, or I try to at least.

Finally, if I really encourage you to find out about the social media accounts that you come coming back to. What do you like about them? Will you remember them? What makes them interesting enough that you keep returning?

I know I don't follow too many social media accounts, but for the ones I do, I have good reasons. For example, USA Today Bestselling author Kristine Kathryn Rusch shares a lot of funny stories, interesting life events and book news that I enjoy looking at. Her cats make us laugh and that's great.

When it comes to Mae Martin's Instagram account, it is always great, funny and fun to see what they're up to as a comedian.

Then in terms of psychology, there are some LinkedIn accounts that I look at on occasion because I know there are a great place to look at if I want certain information on clinical psychology careers and so on.

As a result, I hope this has shown you that social media isn't all bad and it can have benefits for us. It can provide us with a fun, interesting place to learn about the things we're passionate about.

In addition, the entire point of this reflection was to help show you that you might want to cater your professional social media accounts (if you have any) to help form a part of your legacies.

You seriously don't need to be a podcaster, blogger or writer like me. You could be known as someone who posts little inspirational psychology quotes that makes people feel good, you could be known for posting a paragraph a day about your favourite psychology topics, or something else entirely.

If you want to have a digital legacy or even if you just want to use social media more purposefully then maybe be a little more conscious how you post and the type of things you post. We all have ten or more accounts we can randomly think of that we avoid like the plague because they're toxic, awful and their legacies are beyond horrific.

But as future or current clinical psychologists, our social media accounts don't have to be bad or overzealously filled with psychology-related stuff. There is the 80/20 rule so 80% psychology content and 20% personal stuff.

As we move into the new digital age, there will be one question that impacts us more and more, what will your digital legacy be?

COULD INCLUSIVE-LANGUAGE BE IMPORTANT IN THE ADOS AND OTHER MENTAL HEALTH SETTINGS?

Every so often in The Psychologist Magazine by the British Psychological Society, I come across an article that I seriously, seriously like because it's interesting, thought-provoking and it sticks with me for a while after reading it.

I had one of these times when I was reading the November 2022 issue and there was this tiny little article about the Autism Diagnostic Observation Scale because the woman was saying she had watched a training video with her cohort and a five year-old child was asked this question "do you have a girlfriend?" and she acknowledged that the question itself doesn't matter for the clinical task because it is the child's response that is more important than the question. It is to see how the child thinks and responds about human relationships.

Yet I do agree with her point and I will go one

step closer.

For starters, in my personal opinion, why the hell would a 5 year old boy be dating? I don't care if they're dating a boy or girl, why would a 5 year old be dating?

Of course that probably makes me sound hardline or something about children dating, but I think it is weird that we have that sort of expectation. That a kid would be dating and even if they were "dating" they wouldn't know what that really means or the experience that we later experience as teenagers or young adults or adults.

Again I know the question itself isn't important and it is effective for knowing how the child thinks about relationships, a major factor in autism that I am still learning about even now.

The Real Point Of The Article

Getting back onto the real point of the article, the woman is openly gay and she pointed out how the question was strange when we consider the world we live in and the research itself. The original question is "do you have a girlfriend?" and I imagine if the video was about a five year old girl being tested using ADOS, the question would be "do you have a boyfriend?"

Why shouldn't the question be more open and more telling to be honest? The question should be "do you have a girlfriend or boyfriend?"

I think this for three main reasons.

Firstly, I think this is a lot more telling and useful

for the ADOS test itself, because in the event that 5 year old boy (I would still be surprised if a 5 year old was dating) was asked about dating a girl and they weren't, they would just say no and respond a little.

Then depending on the severity of the autism, and judging on my own experiences of even mild autism at that age, chances are if the five year old boy was "dating" another boy then they wouldn't know that they should understand the question is about social relationships and they should reveal and respond on having a boyfriend.

Now at the age of 22, I can understand most of the time the real point behind a question even when it's worded wrong, like this one would be. Yet a five year old wouldn't be able to if they had autism.

Therefore, I strongly believe that the ADOS question was more inclusive by containing those two extra words that might take someone an extra second to say. Then the Scale might get more information to use in the assessment.

And surely, that's the entire point of ADOS?

Important Side Note: No This Will Not Turn Kids Gay

In the very, very rare event that a homophobic person has made it to this section of the book, I can promise you that simply asking a five year old boy "do you have a girlfriend or boyfriend?" will not make them gay. That isn't how it works.

It seriously doesn't.

Also, I think what people need to understand is

kids don't care about gay, straight and everything in-between. They only care about what parents, adults and society tells them later on that this is something to be upset by, disinterested in because you're okay with it and want to support people regardless of their sexuality, or it's perfectly okay and actively encouraged if the person has that interest.

And if they do have an interest in same-sex relationships in the future then you're benefiting them and their mental health by telling them from an early age that it doesn't matter if they like boys or girls.

Because it just doesn't.

<u>Considering The World We Live In</u>

Secondly, we live in a world that is generally more accepting and this is something we need to continue to work on and work towards. And because of the general acceptance, the safety young people feel now and how positive compared to previous decades people are towards LGBT+ people. There are more people in general identifying as LGBT+ and it is still a tiny, tiny minority of the general population, but it is still present.

Therefore, considering psychology is part of the world and society that we want to make more equal, fairer and accepting. It is a little odd that we are implying that opposite-sex relationships are the only options for people at such a young age.

Wouldn't it be a brilliant and such a subtle way to teach children that it's okay to like girls and boys regardless of whatever their preference ends up being?

Just like how we tell girls from a young age that they can do anything they want, they can become engineers, IT people and all the other job roles that are typically male-only. Wouldn't it be good to teach kids the same thing about relationships?

I think it would.

And this would serve two purposes too. It would teach kids if they later discover they're LGBT+ that it's nothing to worry about because you've taught them from that young age that no one cares by asking a simple question in a normal way.

However, for kids that don't discover their LGBT+ then it helps to promote tolerance. Since from that young age you've taught them that it doesn't matter if someone likes boys or girls or both by asking a question in a normal way.

Language has immense power in clinical psychology and so do our questions.

It's A Weird Question Considering The Research

To wrap up this reflection, the original article in The Psychologist mentioned how this was a weird question considering there is an overwhelming amount of research that shows that LGBT+ people are more likely to experience mental health difficulties.

Done that and brought the t-shirt.

Therefore, if we apply this idea of using more inclusive language in other mental health settings and the ADOS itself, then this is only going to benefit people. I know from my own experiences of therapy, it is awful, awkward and just flat out weird to have to "come out" to a therapist because they don't ask things.

It isn't a "normal" or "typical" question in clinical psychology settings.

And considering that a lot of therapists will see LGBT+ people in their practice at some point in their lives because of the mental health difficulties that society and family factors creates for this population. It seems strange that we want to bake into mental health services another factor of distress.

If a therapist had asked me, was I gay and what are my pronouns? I would have bit a little awkward still because of my trauma, abuse and everything that happened to me. Yet it would have been nice to be asked and not have to awkwardly "come out" when explaining why I was there and I was seriously stressed out about it in the time leading up to my first appointment.

Update

In addition, I'm adding this little section in a few hours after writing this reflection because I had my first counselling session at the university, and there is something I want to comment on about this topic.

We were talking about identity and because he didn't ask me anymore about my sexuality and gender identity (because it isn't standard practice), I couldn't really tell him about my trans identity as a non-binary person.

Granted I am not blaming him at all because he is brilliant as well as he knew I was gay anyway because my referral form, and I mentioned it during me talking about why I wanted counselling. Yet since my "new" gender identity (it isn't new at all but I only realised it 6 weeks ago), it was really hard to talk about it and "come out" as a non-binary person.

So I didn't.

And I think I should and it will be helpful but I just felt awkward disclosing it because it is something I am still learning about and that part of myself is still very much developing.

Therefore, my point is that this extremely harmless question of asking "what is your sexuality?" (if it is relevant of course) and "what are your pronouns or what's your gender?" in a therapy setting would be very, very helpful to me in this personal example.

It would have given me an "in" to this disclosing and this is something that all of our clients want at different times. It is no different than clients or therapists building on the comment or conversation the other person has just mentioned.

At the end of the day, psychological therapy is about the exploration of mental health, the client's psychological process and any psychological distress they're experiencing. And all exploration requires us, as future or current psychologists, to have an "in" with a client to start talking about a topic, any topic.

So just in case someone wants to talk or express

or declare their sexuality or gender identity, let's give them the chance. It might be important, it might not be but this would only take an extra 10 seconds.

And that simple question could have immense power, something I talk about more below.

Conclusion

Overall, I strongly believe that inclusive language should be used more in mental health settings, because it isn't hard but the impact could be immense for our clients. It could decrease their psychological distress in the future, it could help promote tolerance in society and it could seriously help put our clients at ease when they first come into our services.

And considering the entire point of clinical psychology is to help our clients improve their lives and decrease their stress. It seems weird that we aren't doing such a simple trick that would only take an extra ten seconds to do but it could have an immensely positive impact for us, the therapeutic alliance and most importantly, our clients.

DO CLINICAL PSYCHOLOGY COMPLAINT PROCEDURES NEED TO BECOME EASIER?

As future or current clinical psychologists, there will be times when we have a client that we aren't a good fit for, we no longer want to see because we don't believe we can help them or we just don't want to see them because we can't work well together.

That is okay because at the end of the day, a therapeutic relationship is a relationship between two different people and sometimes relationships work out. Yet sometimes they do not.

However, I was reading a really good article in the September 2023 edition of The Psychologist about an awful experience that an autistic client had been through were the therapist had said by email that they no longer wanted to see the client. There was no reason given, no explanation and no offer of another service instead.

This was, of course, a private therapist and the

entire article was focused on how damaging this was to the client because there was no more support for them, they couldn't understand why this was done and then when the client tried to find out why. She threatened harassment against the autistic client.

And before I continue I want to jump in here and mention that ending a therapy correctly is flat out critical in clinical psychology. I've reflected on this before in one of the earlier volumes, but if we don't end a therapy correctly then this has immensely damaging effects on a client.

It can even undo all the good work you've done with them over the sessions so the client ends up being back at square one.

Whereas a good ending can leave a client feeling happy, relaxed, engaged and ready to take on the world with their newfound sense of freedom, happiness and their new coping mechanisms. At least that's how I basically felt.

Although, as you can expect this autistic client was really shocked, confused and deeply hurt by the actions of the therapist and this is where we come to the problem within clinical psychology.

Who do you complain to?

Since The British Psychological Society cannot act until they receive an "Unfit To Practice" judgement from the other professional bodies depending on who the person is registered with. As well as the only judgement that can be passed by the other professional organisations is "Unfit To

Practice".

Of course, if you go to the NHS and have a course of therapy through them then I sort of imagine the complaint procedure is easier. Due to you could write to the NHS Trust, NHS England or go to the Department's head.

But when it comes to private therapists in the UK and to be honest aboard. I have no idea.

I know when I had private therapy, I wouldn't have a clue about who to complain to. I didn't even really take note of the three or four professional bodies the therapist was registered too.

Then another problem is that writing to a professional organisation, launching an official complaint and taking part in an investigation takes a hell of a lot of courage. No one likes complaining, no one wants to do this so they only really complain to a professional body if they have the courage to do this.

Not a lot of people do.

In addition, another problem is that "Unfit To Practice". That is an extremely high bar to set when dealing with a complaint and if someone is Unfit To Practice then that leaves a lot potentially questionable behaviour that can go under the radar. All because it doesn't meet the threshold for "Unfit To Practice".

I'm not saying that the therapist was wrong in the article to drop the client, the autistic client wasn't saying that either because they highlighted how there were two sides to every story. Yet the problem remains, in clinical psychology there are no easy ways to complain about a private therapist if they do something "bad" or damaging to a client.

In addition, "Unfit To Practice" is sort of the ultimate punishment too. Most clients don't want a therapist to get struck off just because of one really damaging mistake due to most of these are just one-off mistakes. Yet they want some sort of apology or acknowledgement that what happened was flat out wrong and it should never happen again.

However, because certain actions that have damaging impacts on clients fall below the threshold of "Unfit To Practice" it means that acknowledgement or judgement by a professional governing body never comes.

Personally, I would need to look into this a lot more and the different rules and regulations to make an even more informed judgement on the topic. Yet as someone who has been through therapy twice for different reasons and different things, I think there should be something that isn't quite "Unfit To Practice" but a judgement that means a therapist has to admit what they did in this incident was wrong. It doesn't mean that they were Unfit To Practice, it doesn't mean they're a crap therapist all-around. It just means what they did with a particular person was flat out wrong and it shouldn't have happened in the first place.

Especially as the article in The Psychologist sort of read like everyone was trying to gaslight them into believing being dropped by email by a therapist was perfectly okay, normal and expected.

Is it?

Maybe that is the case, but it doesn't make it morally right considering how we can make clients feel supported in their time of psychological distress. Or at least given them a reason for ending the therapeutic relationship and maybe sign post them to other services that might be able to help them better.

That would at least help stop some of the feelings of abandonment, but this is a very tricky topic that depends on so many different factors between the client and therapist. Yet I do believe complaints within clinical psychology should be easier and more accessible because I think a lot of clients can agree, in the rare incident they need to complain, they have absolutely no idea who to complain to.

And that is dangerous if something does go wrong.

AN UPDATED LOOK AT ENDINGS IN THERAPY

In the last reflection, I spoke about an ending of a therapy that went badly and left the client feeling hurt, damaged and confused about what the hell had gone wrong in the therapy for the therapist to just drop them like that.

In this reflection, I want to reflect on my own personal experience of ending a therapy and how it made me feel as a client. This is useful for all future and current clinical psychologists because it will help you to understand how a client feels coming to the end of a course of therapy that has helped them, transformed their lives and given them hope.

Nonetheless, first of all, I want to include this small extract from CBT For Depression that covers some of the psychological theory behind ending therapy as a whole.

Enjoy.

"How Ending The Therapy Works?

Now this is a critical part of the overall course of treatment because if there is a jerking ending or an unsatisfying end then this can be just as damaging as no therapy at all. For example, one of my lecturers told us how her client had had so many therapists and they just ended up leaving him that it confirmed his cognitive processes about how everyone leaves him in the end.

That isn't what an ending is meant to look like in CBT, so that's why we need to focus on it now. There's no point doing therapy if the ending is only going to undo all the hard work of the client and therapist.

Therefore, the ending of therapy should be like the beginning in terms of it being structured and collaborative. As well as when a therapist does end of a piece with a client they would revisit the goals they set with the client set at the beginning.

To make sure that they've gotten everything they've set out to achieve, and it's nice that you can go to the client, something along the lines of "Look, a few months ago you told me these were all impossible to achieve and now look at you,"

And this links into making the client realise how much *they're* done and why *they're* amazing.

And that's the magic thing about CBT, it is a therapy where the client is always centre-stage because the therapist might give them great tools, but at the end of the day, it is the client that put in the work and made the change all possible.

Sometimes it only takes the skilled hand of a therapist to make them realise just how incredible they actually are."

My Personal Experience of Ending A Therapy

The first major feeling you experience when it comes to ending a therapy is a sort of weird combination of happiness, nervousness and even a little anxiety. Since you're a happy because I was better now and I felt able to go on and live a brilliant life filled with love, healthy relationships and I was pain free for the first time in my life. As well as I was happy I was no longer going to be spending £50 a week on therapy.

I was a little nervous and anxious because ending this therapy meant a major source of psychological support was going to be gone from my life. And that was a very scary thing because I didn't know, or I wasn't sure I was going to be okay with it.

Therefore, your client will most probably have these sort of feelings about ending the therapy regardless of how amazing the work has been. For example, my therapist was flat out amazing and she helped me transform my own life for the better, but I was still experiencing all these different emotions.

Furthermore, when it came to the therapy session, it was really good in the sense that it was very relaxed and we went through a list of about six things that she wanted to wrap up and suggest I continue working on in the future. Since we did some short-term work together and there was more to cover.

I really liked how my therapist just took her time and we spoke about all the different expects of the list she had put together, she warned me against boxing stuff up and it was a good, positive and hopeful therapy session that set me up for the future.

And it's that sense of hope that I really, really liked. She was helping me to realise that I am only 22 and I have my entire life ahead of me. I am going on this massive journey, this massive experience of finding out who I am and everything surrounding me no longer being held back by my pain, trauma and abuse.

She helped me to realise on my own how much hope and great things there are in the future.

Then when it came to ending the final session, she mentioned stuff like how nice it was working together, how interesting it was and there were some empowering reminders about how *I* am the one that did the therapy work and everything like that. I had started therapy as a scared, traumatised, wreck of a person who was spiralling badly.

And I left a new person who was excited about seeing the world for the first-time not through the lens of abuse and trauma.

That's good therapy.

<u>What Does This Mean For Us?</u>

I think for us, as future or current clinical psychologists, it means we need to acknowledge that our clients will be scared, nervous and anxious about the end of psychotherapy. This is normal and it seriously doesn't mean we've done a bad job. This is an extremely normal human experience I think when it comes to ending something that has been so positive and life-changing for them.

Of course, not every client, not every therapist and not every course of therapy will feel this way. If you have not really enjoyed working with a specific client, you might be almost grateful to see them go or your client might never have truly engaged with the therapy.

But as long as we all try our best in psychotherapy then that's okay.

Anyway, I think my experience teaches us that the final session should give the client hope for the future and it should hammer home that we've given the tools to be their own therapists at home and in their life. This means they can go on and live their own lives without having to fall back on their maladaptive coping mechanisms that brought them to our service in the first place.

And to wrap this up, I don't actually think "ending" is the right term to use for this, because yes this is the end of therapy. But it isn't a real end.

In fact, the end of psychotherapy is actually the beginning of something. For me, it was the beginning of being pain-free, being happy and being able to live a life without trauma and abuse controlling every single aspect of myself.

Every client will be different but the end of

therapy isn't the end for a client. It is the beginning of a journey towards a new and exciting and hopeful life filled with joys, wonders and a lot of happiness.

But sometimes it takes us giving the client a few reminders to make them realise it.

https://www.subscribepage.io/gayromancesignup

https://www.subscribepage.io/psychologyboxset

CHECK OUT THE PSYCHOLOGY WORLD PODCAST FOR MORE PSYCHOLOGY INFORMATION! AVAILABLE ON ALL MAJOR PODCAST APPS.

About the author:

Connor Whiteley is the author of over 60 books in the sci-fi fantasy, nonfiction psychology and books for writer's genre and he is a Human Branding Speaker and Consultant.

He is a passionate warhammer 40,000 reader, psychology student and author.

Who narrates his own audiobooks and he hosts The Psychology World Podcast.

All whilst studying Psychology at the University of Kent, England.

Also, he was a former Explorer Scout where he gave a speech to the Maltese President in August 2018 and he attended Prince Charles' 70th Birthday Party at Buckingham Palace in May 2018.

Plus, he is a self-confessed coffee lover!

All books in 'An Introductory Series':
Careers In Psychology
Psychology of Suicide
Dementia Psychology
Clinical Psychology Reflections Volume 4
Forensic Psychology of Terrorism And Hostage-Taking
Forensic Psychology of False Allegations
Year In Psychology
CBT For Anxiety
CBT For Depression
Applied Psychology
BIOLOGICAL PSYCHOLOGY 3RD EDITION
COGNITIVE PSYCHOLOGY THIRD EDITION
SOCIAL PSYCHOLOGY- 3RD EDITION
ABNORMAL PSYCHOLOGY 3RD EDITION
PSYCHOLOGY OF RELATIONSHIPS- 3RD EDITION
DEVELOPMENTAL PSYCHOLOGY 3RD EDITION
HEALTH PSYCHOLOGY
RESEARCH IN PSYCHOLOGY
A GUIDE TO MENTAL HEALTH AND TREATMENT AROUND THE WORLD-

A GLOBAL LOOK AT DEPRESSION
FORENSIC PSYCHOLOGY
THE FORENSIC PSYCHOLOGY OF THEFT, BURGLARY AND OTHER CRIMES AGAINST PROPERTY
CRIMINAL PROFILING: A FORENSIC PSYCHOLOGY GUIDE TO FBI PROFILING AND GEOGRAPHICAL AND STATISTICAL PROFILING.
CLINICAL PSYCHOLOGY FORMULATION IN PSYCHOTHERAPY
PERSONALITY PSYCHOLOGY AND INDIVIDUAL DIFFERENCES
CLINICAL PSYCHOLOGY REFLECTIONS VOLUME 1
CLINICAL PSYCHOLOGY REFLECTIONS VOLUME 2
Clinical Psychology Reflections Volume 3
CULT PSYCHOLOGY
Police Psychology

A Psychology Student's Guide To University
How Does University Work?
A Student's Guide To University And Learning
University Mental Health and Mindset

Other books by Connor Whiteley:

Bettie English Private Eye Series

A Very Private Woman
The Russian Case
A Very Urgent Matter
A Case Most Personal
Trains, Scots and Private Eyes
The Federation Protects
Cops, Robbers and Private Eyes
Just Ask Bettie English
An Inheritance To Die For
The Death of Graham Adams
Bearing Witness
The Twelve
The Wrong Body
The Assassination Of Bettie English
Wining And Dying
Eight Hours
Uniformed Cabal
A Case Most Christmas

Gay Romance Novellas

Breaking, Nursing, Repairing A Broken Heart
Jacob And Daniel
Fallen For A Lie
Spying And Weddings
Clean Break

Awakening Love
Meeting A Country Man
Loving Prime Minister
Snowed In Love
Never Been Kissed
Love Betrays You

Lord of War Origin Trilogy:
Not Scared Of The Dark
Madness
Burn Them All

The Fireheart Fantasy Series
Heart of Fire
Heart of Lies
Heart of Prophecy
Heart of Bones
Heart of Fate

City of Assassins (Urban Fantasy)
City of Death
City of Martyrs
City of Pleasure
City of Power

Agents of The Emperor
Return of The Ancient Ones
Vigilance
Angels of Fire
Kingmaker
The Eight
The Lost Generation
Hunt
Emperor's Council
Speaker of Treachery
Birth Of The Empire
Terraforma
Spaceguard

The Rising Augusta Fantasy Adventure Series
Rise To Power
Rising Walls
Rising Force
Rising Realm

Lord Of War Trilogy (Agents of The Emperor)
Not Scared Of The Dark
Madness
Burn It All Down

Miscellaneous:
RETURN
FREEDOM
SALVATION
Reflection of Mount Flame
The Masked One
The Great Deer
English Independence

OTHER SHORT STORIES BY CONNOR WHITELEY

Mystery Short Story Collections
Criminally Good Stories Volume 1: 20 Detective Mystery Short Stories
Criminally Good Stories Volume 2: 20 Private Investigator Short Stories
Criminally Good Stories Volume 3: 20 Crime Fiction Short Stories
Criminally Good Stories Volume 4: 20 Science Fiction and Fantasy Mystery Short Stories
Criminally Good Stories Volume 5: 20 Romantic Suspense Short Stories

<u>Mystery Short Stories:</u>
Protecting The Woman She Hated
Finding A Royal Friend
Our Woman In Paris
Corrupt Driving
A Prime Assassination
Jubilee Thief
Jubilee, Terror, Celebrations
Negative Jubilation
Ghostly Jubilation
Killing For Womenkind
A Snowy Death
Miracle Of Death
A Spy In Rome
The 12:30 To St Pancreas
A Country In Trouble
A Smokey Way To Go
A Spicy Way To GO
A Marketing Way To Go
A Missing Way To Go
A Showering Way To Go
Poison In The Candy Cane
Kendra Detective Mystery Collection Volume 1
Kendra Detective Mystery Collection Volume 2
Mystery Short Story Collection Volume 1

CLINICAL PSYCHOLOGY REFLECTIONS VOLUME 5

Mystery Short Story Collection Volume 2
Criminal Performance
Candy Detectives
Key To Birth In The Past

Science Fiction Short Stories:
Their Brave New World
Gummy Bear Detective
The Candy Detective
What Candies Fear
The Blurred Image
Shattered Legions
The First Rememberer
Life of A Rememberer
System of Wonder
Lifesaver
Remarkable Way She Died
The Interrogation of Annabella Stormic
Blade of The Emperor
Arbiter's Truth
Computation of Battle
Old One's Wrath
Puppets and Masters
Ship of Plague
Interrogation
Edge of Failure

<u>Fantasy Short Stories:</u>
City of Snow
City of Light
City of Vengeance
Dragons, Goats and Kingdom
Smog The Pathetic Dragon
Don't Go In The Shed
The Tomato Saver
The Remarkable Way She Died
Dragon Coins
Dragon Tea
Dragon Rider

www.ingramcontent.com/pod-product-compliance
Lightning Source LLC
LaVergne TN
LVHW012108070526
838202LV00056B/5664